£3

C000020805

NORFOLK

Wroxham Broad, 1961. This wonderful expanse of water is about 100 acres in extent, about 1 mile long and 100 yards wide. It has been host to pleasurecraft and waterborne sports since long before the Broads gained mass popularity. Water frolics are recorded here as early as the eighteenth century. By the early years of the twentieth century the frolics had been transformed into more formal regattas, the most important of which was usually held here on 1 and 2 August. What a sight these early regattas must have been with the whole broad bedecked with bunting and craft displaying bright flag signals, all crews turned out in their best flannels, ladies in their prettiest dresses. The competition would begin at 11.00 a.m. Each competition in various classes of craft entailed navigating a course of ten circuits of the broad, yachts completing the rounds in about two hours. Competitions and regattas are still held on the broad. To the left of the water is the headquarters clubhouse and moorings of the Norfolk Broads Yacht Club.

HISTORIC BRITAIN *from the Air*

NORFOLK

NEIL R. STOREY

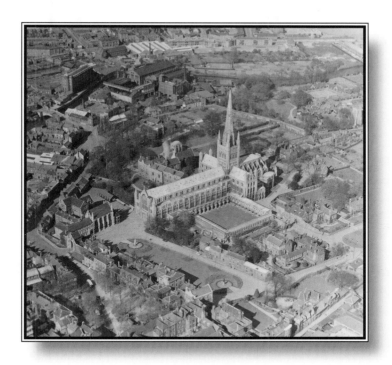

SUTTON PUBLISHING

First published in the United Kingdom in 1999 by Sutton Publishing Limited · Phoenix Mill · Thrupp · Stroud · Gloucestershire · GL5 2BU

British Library Cataloguing in Publication Data
A catalogue record for this book is available from the British Library.

ISBN 0-7509-1936-1

Half title page photograph: Castle Rising, 1948.
Title page photograph: Norwich Cathedral, 1939.

Typeset in 11/14pt Photina.
Typesetting and origination by Sutton Publishing Limited.
Printed in Great Britain by The Bath Press, Bath.

> This book is dedicated to my mother, Diane who introduced me to and shared her affection for the historic corners, byways and folklore of Norfolk on our summer holiday travels around the county when I was a boy.

Acknowledgements

I wish to record my sincere thanks to the following who have kindly and generously assisted me in the compilation of this book: Basil Gowan, Philip Standley, Eric Reading, Chris Cock, Carolyn Barclay, Norfolk Windmills Trust, Richard Wine at BP Amoco, Reg West, Maggie Secker, Andy Archer, all the contributing listeners at BBC Radio Norfolk, readers of Eastern Counties Newspapers, and the ECN Library Staff.

A special thanks must go to John Fendick for showing me the county from the air (for real) and further special thanks are warmly extended to all staff at the Norfolk Studies Library at the Norwich Central Library who, no matter how long the list, diversity or obscurity of my enquiries, have done their very best to help me.

I am also grateful to Nick Walmsley, Editor of *Dirigible*, for his help with the caption for the picture of Pulham airship base on p. 38.

As ever this book has been a team effort and I wish to express my thanks to all who have contacted me with 'snippets' of information or who have simply called to wish me well with my project. This book has been like a multi-discipline degree to me and those kind words have gone a long way to help me 'keep a'troshin''.

Finally, but certainly by no means least, I give heartfelt thanks to my family, old and new, for their encouragement and support throughout. Thanks in particular to my darling wife Sarah for the additional research work and her enduring love for this temperamental author.

Contents

Great Yarmouth, 1969. Today 3 miles of boating lakes, waterways, ornamental gardens, putting greens, bowling greens, amusement arcades and funfairs make up Great Yarmouth seafront. It is hard to imagine all this land as wide open drying ground for fishermen's nets and the town confined within its walls as it once was. The vogue for 'taking waters' extended to bathing in the eighteenth century. In 1759 the bath-house was built to exploit this idea and by the 1830s it had developed into a hotel. Other properties sprung up with entrepreneurs cashing in on the fashion. The seafront gradually began to take shape reflecting the in vogue Regency styles of Brighton and the Italianate style of the Victorians. The fashion of promenading was extended to walks over the beach and even out over the sea on the old jetty. Then the Wellington Pier was constructed in 1853 and the Britannia Pier followed in 1857. All three structures have endured extensions, major alterations and additions but still exist today.

Introduction

Over the years it has been my pleasure and privilege to see some of the finest collections of topographical postcards and photographs of Norfolk in the past. Such views constantly prove to me the truth of the old maxim that 'a picture speaks a thousand words'. They reflect not only the way places used to look but also how our forebears lived, worked and entertained themselves. Only from the aerial viewpoint is it really possible to consider, quite literally, the wider angle on life, to observe the changing and developing face of the whole county of Norfolk set in its geographical context.

The first glimpses of Norfolk from the air were obtained when Mr Dekker brought his royal balloon to Quantrell's Rural Gardens in Norwich in 1785. Spectators paid 10s 6d for front seats or 5s for a place in the second row to watch the ascent and view the balloon and the gondola. Such ascents soon became a popular form of entertainment.

After the advent of powered flight, pioneered by the Wright Brothers in 1903, the enthusiasm for and development of aircraft grew apace. Airmen raced to be the first to fly over national landmarks and to cross seas, often for great rewards, trophies and popular acclaim. The first man to fly over Norwich was Mr Bentfield C. Hucks. He made the journey on 3 August 1912 in the *Daily Mail* monoplane, 'Firefly', while on a promotional tour of the country. In the 70hp Blériot monoplane he set off from Crowhurst Farm, Gorleston, to land near Church Lane, Eaton.

In the same year the Royal Flying Corps was formed. Other European powers were also beginning to realise the strategic military importance of aircraft and started to develop their own air forces, most notable among these being the German naval airship division which was also raised in 1912.

From this time land was acquired across Great Britain for development as airfields by the defence ministries. One of the first purchases, made in strict secrecy, was at Pulham St Mary where No. 2 Coastal Airship Station (Pulham) was opened in 1916 (see page 38).

In 1913 people across Norfolk had wondered at the huge, hovering Zeppelins that skirted the county. It did not take much imagination to see these massive craft as aerial battleships that could be used for malevolent purposes and people in Norfolk did

Bentfield C. Hucks, the first man to fly over Norwich, 3 August 1912.

The University of East Anglia, 1969. The first university buildings on this site were built by Denys Lasdun & Partners in 1962 over the old municipal golf course. Some of the bunkers, dug out and planted with trees, may be observed around the newly built campus grounds. The idea behind the construction of the UEA was to integrate student accommodation with the teaching blocks themselves. When this picture was taken only the ziggurats (the stepped buildings), chemistry and biology blocks were standing. They are now connected to form the main teaching area, five and six storeys high, built of Trent concrete zigzagging east to west across the site. Other buildings, including the Sainsbury Centre for the arts and a variety of schools, have been developed across the campus. The overgrown gravel pit in the foreground, beside the bend of the River Yare, was flooded in the 1970s to form a great lake and has now become a fine habitat for all manner of wildlife.

not have to wait long to have their suspicions confirmed. On 19 January 1915 Zeppelins carried out the first aerial assault on a civilian target in the history of warfare. They raided the coastal towns of Sheringham, Great Yarmouth, Snettisham and King's Lynn, dropping high explosive and incendiary bombs, which killed five people and injured hundreds of others. It later transpired that the Zeppelin crews believed they were attacking key military installations around the Humber Estuary. As a consequence of this and similar disastrous actions during the First World War, aerial photography was developed by both sides as a means of reconnaissance. By 1918 the new technique had become a science in its own right and was firmly established as an essential tool of military intelligence.

In 1919 Mr F.L. Wills, an architect who had gained flying experience in the Royal Naval Air Service, founded Aerofilms, the first commercial aerial photographic business in the UK. In a specially converted three-seater de Havilland DH9 Mr Wills, his pilot and a heavy plate camera operator flew photographic sorties all over the country.

Drawing on Aerofilm's comprehensive library of over 1.5 million images, which date from negative no. 1 of 1919 to the present day, it has been possible to assemble a unique and fascinating portrait of Norfolk, its features, settlements and city, covering sixty years of change, development and growth. I am sure all readers will find places in these pages that they are very familiar with. But Aerofilms' images show the familiar from a very unfamiliar viewpoint and also record areas of the county that have completely changed during the twentieth century or have even been swept away by time and tide. Thanks to the remarkable clarity and quality of the photographs herein, we are able to view these places and structures in their entirety. Norwich can be seen in a series of contrasting pictures that reveal the city dotted with factories, chimneys and breweries, then gutted by the 'Baedeker blitz' of 1942, before being reconstructed and developed during the postwar years (see pages 61–7).

Coastal erosion, which is a constant concern for those who live by the soft cliffs of North Norfolk, is also clearly reflected in the photographs. They cause me to recall the words of a very old Norfolk farm labourer whom I met when I was a young lad out cycling near Walcott with my Grandfather. He reminisced that in his childhood there was once another road closer to the sea than the one on which we were travelling. Beyond the second road, he remembered, there was once a huge field of barley that he had helped to harvest. I could scarcely believe him but his words have stuck with me. All these years later, observing the deterioration of our coast in these photographs, his words have a whole new ring of truth.

I hope this book will enable readers to observe Norfolk from a whole new perspective in every sense. Life did once move at a slower pace, and the settlements of the county did retain their ancient form up until a time well within living memory, as some of these images show. The history in our surroundings belongs to all of us; it is an integral part of our culture, language and identity. It is up to us to preserve what is left for generations to come. No one should be shamed for standing up to those who propose change for change's or 'modernisation's' sake. It is worth remembering that our history in the landscape and structures around us can be lost forever with the fall of the demolition mace or the construction of another housing estate, when it could have been saved by the pen.

Neil R. Storey, North Walsham, October 1999

A Changing & Historic Landscape

Scolt Head Island, 1968. This sand spit between Brancaster Bay and Holkham Bay has been subjected to constant change brought about by the forces of nature. It began to form about 4,000 years ago at the mouth of the estuary just beyond the salt marshes. As the longshore currents sweep deposits along with them, they encourage the development of sand banks and the mud flats that lie in the calmer waters behind them. This is a site of outstanding interest to naturalists and particularly ornithologists: there is an internationally renowned ternery on the brow of the spit and all manner of unusual birds may be observed here throughout the year. This area has been preserved thanks mostly to the vision, studies and investment of Professor F.W. Oliver and Dr S.H. Long at the beginning of the twentieth century. Most of the site was handed to the National Trust in 1923. The Norfolk Naturalists Trust purchased the remainder, formerly retained by Lord Leicester, in 1945.

Two views of The Wash, 1959. Winding creeks and channels cut their silvery way across the sands. Here four rivers – the Ouse, Nene, Welland and Witham – cross the ancient wetlands and flow into the estuary. The Wash is bounded by Hunstanton Point, on the Norfolk Coast, and Wainfleet Point, on the Lincolnshire coast. It is nearly 17 miles long and 13 wide, having an area of 230 square miles. About two-thirds of this extent is dry at low water during spring tides and the remainder varies from 5 to 16 fathoms deep.

The unpredictability of this landscape has been 'discovered' to the misfortune of many a weary traveller, most notoriously King John. He first visited Bishop's Lynn in 1204 and granted its first Royal Charter, making it a borough. Leaving after his second visit in 1216 he headed for Newark, Nottinghamshire, on the long way round via Wisbech. His baggage train of equipment and valuables set off across The Wash to arrive before him, and while crossing a causeway, as folklore tells, the whole entourage was swept away by waves and engulfed by the quicksands, never to be seen again.

Broome Heath, Ditchingham, 1948. The lozenge-shaped mound on the left is an example of an intact Neolithic long barrow (burial mound). The survival of these structures is rare in Norfolk; most of those that did exist in the county have now been lost, having been flattened by agricultural activity over the years. This area also has Bronze Age round barrows, visible to the right, and no doubt this site was of immense sacred, mystical and ritualistic importance to the ancients.

Caistor St Edmund, the site of Venta Icenorum, 1953. In the summer drought of 1928 a pilot flying over Caistor noticed a curious yet regular grid pattern of pale parched corn contrasted against the green barley fields on land between the church and River Tas. The photographs taken a few days later were interpreted to reveal the layout of the Roman town of Venta Icenorum, and an article about the site was published in *The Times* in 1929.

Venta Icenorum had been the tribal capital of the Iceni who controlled Norfolk and most of Suffolk during the Bronze Age. When the Romans conquered the area they adopted it as their regional capital too. A great deal of local and national interest was directed towards the newly discovered site, and further aerial photographs were taken. Archaeological excavations were then carried out in 1929 and 1935 by Professor Donald Atkinson. These revealed a great deal more about the extent to which the Romans built the town anew. The foundations and remains of many significant buildings that once stood on the site, including the fortified gates, forum, temples, quayside and public baths, were all uncovered. Good trade routes were essential, and it is interesting to note that some of the roads built to link Caistor with other towns and settlements are still in use 2,000 years later. A good example is the A140 to Norwich which follows the line of the Roman road that once led from Caistor to the major Roman towns of Colchester and London. After the Romans left the town gradually fell into decline, but a new settlement on the banks of the Wensum gained importance between the seventh and ninth centuries when administrative power was transferred there. That town was Northwic, which grew to become the present city of Norwich.

Thetford Castle, 1928. The great castle mound rises 80 feet in height (but the walk up the slope is 100 feet long) and 1,000 feet round the base. This structure began as an Iron Age fort consisting of a double bank and ditch, creating a defensive strongpoint from which to keep a watch over the junction of the Thet and the Little Ouse. It is here that the prehistoric track, the Icknield Way, crosses the river. Granted to William de Warenne by William the Conqueror, the old fort was converted to a motte and bailey castle, probably constructed in wood. By the middle of the twelfth century the castle had fallen into disuse and it is believed the king ordered its demolition. No further castle was built.

Little Walsingham, 1950. In 1061 Richeldis, the young widow of Ricoldie de Faverches, had a vision in which the Virgin Mary showed her the Holy House, scene of the Annunciation in Nazareth, telling her to mark well the length and breadth and to build an exact replica at Walsingham. Richeldis duly built the first little chapel, similar to the Santa Casa at Nazareth, here. Her son Geoffrey endowed it with lands and founded a priory of Austin Canons to which he gave the chapel of St Mary. With the exception of Thomas à Becket's shrine at Canterbury, no site of pilgrimage in the land was more visited. The most precious of the many relics at the shrine was some of the Virgin's milk. The road to Little Walsingham became one of England's great highways but it took a great deal of work to change its name to the Walsingham Way from the vulgar nickname it had been given – 'the Milky Way'! For 500 years monarchs and humble pilgrims alike made journeys here. The last English King to visit was Henry VIII, who was to destroy it a few years later. All that may be seen of this great priory today are a few ruinous fragments: the most notable, visible just above centre of the photograph, is the fifteenth-century east end of the priory church. The majestic arch of the great window can be seen; above it in the gable is a round window, and at each side a turret with niches in buttresses.

Thetford Priory, 1946. As Thetford's early military significance declined its importance as a religious centre grew. From 1075 it was the seat of the bishopric until Herbert de Losinga moved it to Norwich and began his great cathedral there. The Priory of Our Lady was founded by Roger Bigod in about 1104 as a Cluniac monastery. After its initial site proved too small it moved to its new position here at the bottom of Minstergate. At the dissolution in 1536 there were thirteen monks and revenues estimated at £316 per annum. In this picture the outline of a Romanesque church, monastic buildings and a fourteenth-century, two-storey gateway are clearly visible. Just above middle left is Abbey Farm whose buildings still stand today. However, its field land beyond is now a housing estate.

Castle Acre, 1971. This was one of many estates granted by William I to William de Warenne after the Norman Conquest. De Warenne constructed a great country house and courtyard surrounded by a palisaded bank and defensive ditch on the site. In about 1140 this was converted into a keep and the defences strengthened to create a stronghold that could establish firm control over the nearby river crossing over the Nar and oversee the course of the Peddars Way. By the twelfth century this had become one of the largest castle earthworks in England, spreading over some 15 acres. The growing village was defended by a ditch and walled bank with two entrances straddled by gatehouses. Most of the defences' course is denoted by the tree line seen surrounding the village on the photograph. The castle had fallen into decline by the fourteenth century, and most of its site has been given over to pasturage by 1347. The stone from the decaying ruin was used in the construction of new and improved houses in the village. Excavated in 1976, the site of the castle has yielded many of its ancient secrets and is well worth a visit today.

Castle Rising, 1948. Here we can observe the 120 feet tall earthwork and Norman keep which formed a great defensive work built by the D'Albini family on lands given to them after the Norman Conquest. After Queen Isabella had been convicted of connivance in the murder of Richard II in 1328 she was confined within these castle walls, and was visited there by her son Edward III and her grandson the 'Black Prince'. By 1397 the building had ceased to be a residence and fell into decay, along with the village, as the sea channel receded. The silting up of the waterway led to the old rhyme 'Rising was a seaport, when Lynn it was a marsh. Now Lynn is a seaport and Rising fares the warse.' In 1614 Henry Howard, Earl of Northampton, gave the Bede Houses for twelve 'poor women' and their governess to the village and quietly the village began to repopulate with a few neat cottages being built. Most of the houses seen in the village today, however, are under 200 years old. Slightly to the left of the picture and behind the castle is the church of St Lawrence. It incorporates Norman and Early English styles but its distinctive tower with saddle back roof and belfry were constructed during restoration work in the mid-nineteenth century.

The site of Bromholm Priory, Bacton, 1950. These few humble ruins can barely give an impression of the once great monastic house that stood here. Founded by William de Glanville in 1113, it was built as a cell to Castle Acre Priory for Cluniac monks. At first quite poor, its fortunes changed after 1205 when it proudly claimed to hold a portion of the True Cross. The relic had been brought to this country by an English priest who had obtained the pieces along with some other remains from the Emperor's Chapel in Constantinople. The relics were sold to other religious houses with the exception of the cross fragments which were believed to be fake. At length he came to Bromholm and showed the prior and brethren the relic, which was constructed of two pieces laid across each other and was as wide as a man's hand. The priest gave it to the prior in exchange for his admission to the priory. This object was placed with reverence in the oratory and a strange series of well-attested miracles began: the blind had their sight restored; the lame walked; lepers were 'made clean'; and devils were released from the possessed. These phenomena attracted national acclaim and interest. Visited by Edward III (1327–77) with his court, Bromholm became part of the East Anglian 'Pilgrim's Way'. Its fortunes had changed and it was greatly extended to include a new chapter house, dormitory and 200 foot shrine for the Cross, whose fame had spread to popular language. The Miller's Wife in *The Canterbury Tales* cries 'Helpe, Holy Cross of Bromholm' and Piers Plowman exclaims 'Bidde the Roode of Bromholm bring me out of dette.' Bromholm fell at the dissolution with most of the other monasteries in 1536 – but what of its potent relic? Some say it was lost after it was sent to the King's minister Thomas Cromwell in London; some suggest it was burnt along with the rood. But I prefer believe that it was buried nearby and still waits to be recovered and revered again.

New Buckenham Castle, 1953. These are the remains of the earliest shell keep in England. It dates from 1146 when William D'Albini founded this new fortification and settlement, endowed with a market. He gave Old Buckenham to the Augustinian monks to prevent the new foundation being held against him. This area is almost unique because to this day the village retains the grid layout distinctive of a medieval planned town, and has remained within its original boundaries. These are marked by the town ditch, parts of which were widened in the nineteenth century to serve the village's tanning industry.

Middleton Towers, 1956. This often forgotten, grand stately home, has a moat and a fifteenth-century gatehouse with four turret towers and an oriel window. It was begun by Thomas, Lord Scales. A loyal Lancastrian, he was killed in 1460 by Thames watermen as he made his escape from the Tower of London. He was succeeded at Middleton by his son-in-law, Anthony Woodville, later Lord Rivers, who completed the building. But Rivers met an ignominious end too when he was beheaded without trial by Richard III in 1483. Passing through various families, the hall slowly fell into disrepair until it was considerably restored and enlarged in 1860. Further rebuilding work was undertaken in 1900.

Wallington Hall, 1962. The house is situated in the tiny combined parishes of Wallington-cum-Thorpland and during the reign of Henry VIII (1509–47), when Wallington was a town, it was the seat of the Coningsbys, passing by marriage during the reign of Elizabeth I (1558–1603) to the Gawdy family. The property then went to Judge Gawdy (Chief Justice of the Common Pleas) who set about depopulating the town so that he could have a park. He even converted the nearby church of St Margaret into a hay store and dog kennel. The only part of the church now remaining is the tower seen to the upper right of the photograph. Gawdy reduced Wallington to a one house town – his. However, his comeuppance came when his corpse was brought from London to Wallington. As he had effectively disposed of his local church, the bearers could find no place for his burial. His body ' . . . growing very offensive' was at last conveyed to Runcton church where it was buried without ceremony.

Stiffkey Hall, 1951. This house was bought by Sir Nicholas Bacon, half-brother of Francis Bacon, the essayist, and Queen Elizabeth's Lord Keeper of the Great Privy Seal in 1571. Probably having never seen it, he died in 1577 leaving the house and money to improve and enlarge it to his second son, Sir Nathaniel Bacon. The finished building was a large, castellated mansion, built round three sides of a courtyard with massive circular towers at the corners; the fourth side on the south had a wall with a gatehouse in the centre and the gardens were terraced down to the river. Nathaniel lived until 1615; seven years earlier he had had a memorial built for his body in the nearby church. He left the hall, in the absence of a male heir, to his daughter Anne, the widow of Sir Roger Townshend. Their son Roger carried on the fine family building tradition with the construction of the magnificent Raynham Hall. Today all that is left of Stiffkey Hall is the western and part of the northern range, along with the connecting round towers; the rest is ruins or simply an outline marked by the outer limits of the lawn.

Fenland south of Downham Market, 1962. This area saw the first concerted attempt to drain the southern peat fens to create manageable farmland. The idea came from the Earl of Bedford backed by thirteen 'adventurers'; they appointed the experienced Dutch engineer Cornelius Vermuyden to guide the project and between 1634 and 1653 he reclaimed thousands of acres of fenland by cutting the Bedford and Hundred Foot rivers. The parallel channels, each 21 miles long, confined a great reservoir for winter floodwater known as 'The Washes'. The size of this scheme may be judged when you consider the area covered was equal to seven-fifths of the total area reclaimed in the Netherlands between 1540 and 1690.

Heydon Hall, 1950. This beautiful manor house was built between 1581 and 1584 by Henry Dynne, an auditor of the exchequer during the reign of Elizabeth I. After his death it was sold to the Colfers, who in turn sold it to the Kemps, who sold it to Erasmus Earle, MP for Norwich in the Long Parliament and Sergeant-at-Law to Oliver Cromwell. Earle was one of those who met at Uxbridge in January 1645 to negotiate matters between the King and Parliament. It is said that on one of his visits to Heydon, Cromwell was charged by an enraged bull. The Lord Protector was saved by climbing a mighty oak near the hall, and the tree was known thereafter as Cromwell's Oak.

The Earles were at Heydon for over 100 years until the male line died out in 1762 and the house was sold to the Bulwer family. It passed through several generations of Bulwers and was enlarged with extensions and towers in the 1840s and '50s by William Bulwer to become the edifice seen in this photograph. Since the property passed into the hands of William Bulwer Long the unmanageable Victorian additions have been removed, and the building is now looking very much as it did in the time of Henry Dynne.

Holkham Hall, 1951. In the seventeenth century the Coke family acquired the entire parish of Holkham by means of fortunate marriages and opportune purchases. They created a great park, 9 miles round, enclosing 3,200 acres of which 1,100 were wooded. Here in 1734 the great house was begun by Thomas Coke. Designed by William Kent and Matthew Brettingham – and with input and overall supervision from Thomas himself – it is one of the finest examples of the Palladian style of architecture in the country. It was this Thomas Coke who began the agricultural reforms on his estate. It was he who turned a waste of sheep walks into rich arable lands. He died in 1759 and his widow completed the building in 1760. On her death in 1766 it passed for a few months to her nephew until he died and his son Thomas William Coke inherited the estate. He truly secured the future of his family fortunes and ensured 'Coke of Holkham', would go down in history as a national agricultural reformer. His great farming innovations employed across the estate ranged from incorporating an insistance on new improved farming methods in tenant farmer lease agreements to the establishment of his famous 'Holkham Shearings' – the forerunner of modern agricultural shows.

Sall Park, 1968. A short distance from this house stood the ancient home of the Nugouns, Lords of the Manor during the reign of King John. After the Nugouns the land passed to the Briggs, Fountains and Hases. Nugouns Manor was demolished to clear the park for the Georgian brick mansion seen here, built in 1761 for Edward Hase after his wife Vertue Repps had inherited the manor. This great house with seven bays and two-and-a-half storeys was built in the Palladian tradition. It is set in 250 acres of parkland. It was restored in 1862 and two-storey service blocks were added in 1910 for Sir Woolmer White. Extensive interior alterations were carried out the same year. This magnificent building, so typical of the surviving great country houses of Norfolk, still stands proud today.

Sandringham House, 1932. A house owned variously by the families of Clifton, Scales, Cobbe and Hoste stood on this site for hundreds of years. In 1752 Susan, the last of the senior line of Hoste, married Cornish Hensley. Upon inheriting the property their son pulled down the manor, not leaving any trace of the old building, and built a regency house. When it left his hands it was greatly altered by the flamboyant Victorian architect Samuel Teulon. In 1862 Queen Victoria was looking for a country house for her son, Edward, Prince of Wales, who was coming of age and to be married. She was offered Sandringham for £220,000, a price which she accepted. Extensive changes were planned and the present building was designed by A.J. Humbert and completed in 1870. The beautiful gardens were laid out by W.B. Thomas. After a fire damaged part of the building in 1891 a small extension was designed by R.W. Edis. Little has changed since then apart from the demolition of a wing in 1976. It is still the Norfolk residence of HM The Queen, and the royal family traditionally spend their New Year holiday on the estate.

Land reclaimed from The Wash near King's Lynn, 1955. In 1837 an extensive plan was drawn up for the reclamation of 150,000 acres of land from The Wash. This new land, about the size of Rutland, was to be known as 'Victoria County'. The group behind the plan became known as the Norfolk Estuary Company and by 1848, when government approval was given, it included the eminent engineers Sir John Rennie and Robert Stephenson and was headed by Lord William Bentinck and Sir William Ffolkes. Work commenced in 1850 and construction of the new drainage cut went well until a dispute occurred between investors and a legal wrangle ensued. This seriously hampered an already expensive project. The dream was not to be. Over the last 100 years only 4,000 acres were reclaimed by the Norfolk Estuary Company and about 3,500 by others.

Easton Lodge, 1938. Built in the 1770s to command an excellent view over Easton Heath, it was formerly the lodge of the gamekeeper to Costessey Manor. Under the ownership of Thomas Trench Berney it was extended and expertly fronted in the classic Georgian style. In the early nineteenth century it was described as 'an elegant modern mansion'. It was home in 1845 to Colonel Richard Montagu Oakes, the first Chief Constable of Norfolk (1840–52). Over the years Easton Lodge was occupied by various local gentry, farmers and landowners. At the time this photograph was taken it was home to Colin Kidner, one of the principal landowners in Easton at the time.

When Easton Hall was sold in 1948 it was described as a 'Residential, Agricultural and Sporting Estate' with 200 acres of woodland, trout stream, an established shoot, farmhouse, poultry farm and six estate cottages, in all adding up to about 485 acres. Today Easton Lodge is owned by Mr John Rampton who keenly maintains the traditions and trades of the old estate, assisted in the conservation work by his son Matthew. The gardens of this magnificent house are open to the public once a year in mid-July as part of the National Gardens Scheme.

Aylsham Poor Law Institution, 1932. Following the growing demands on the Aylsham Union of forty-five parishes to provide a 'House of Industry' of its own, in lieu of the workhouses at Buxton and Oulton, this handsome brick building was built on Cawston Road in 1849. The Elizabethan-style institution cost £12,000 and had facilities for 619 inmates. It accommodated paupers (including children), numbering roughly 100 at any one time, from the surrounding parishes. If they were able-bodied they would work for their keep or would be confined to the infirmary if sick or infirm. In 1929 the Board of Guardians passed the management of the Poor Law Institution to Norfolk County Council who ran it on much the same lines as the previous regime. At the time this photograph was taken Benjamin Sapwell was the Master, Ronald Victor Rylance was the Medical Officer and the Revd Edward Dennis was Chaplain.

In 1948 the whole property was taken over by the National Health Service and gradually the whole building was adapted to become the present St Michael's Hospital. The last of the workhouse 'inmates' were placed in council homes.

West Runton, 1950. These earthworks are one of a pair of old rifle butts situated a short distance apart off Water Lane near Woman Hithe on the cliff path at West Runton. They date from about 1914 and were used by locally stationed troops during training and on coastal defence duties during the First World War. Shortly after 1918 they were made redundant, and have become overgrown and enigmatic features near the cliff edge.

Pulham airship base, 1926. Plans for this airship base were begun in secret in 1912 and it was commissioned by the Admiralty as No. 2 Coastal Airship Station in 1916 when the Submarine Scout non-rigid type airships flew their first 'active' patrols over the North Sea. These blimps became know as 'Pulham Pigs'. The base's first shed (the smaller building, above centre) was made of wood by Messrs Hippersons – from a German design! The first large shed, No. 1, is on the right of the pair. Its 90 feet doors were built of iron and steel, and were operated by manual capstans. Some 350–400 personnel were required to catch and cling to the holding ropes of the airships as they came in and then walk the vessels back to the sheds. Initially the gas for the airships was brought to the station in large cylinders, but in 1916 Pulham began producing its own hydrogen; the manufacturing plant is visible between the big sheds and the gas holders, which are to the right of the centre of the photograph. The great airships R33, R36 and R80 were all based at Pulham. The base was decommissioned in 1926 when the centre of airship operations moved to Cardington in Bedfordshire. Pulham's No. 2 shed (the left one of the large pair) was also transported to Cardington where it housed R100; the shed is still there. No. 1 shed was demolished and some of its material may have been used in the construction of The Firs stadium in Norwich. The main role of the airfield during the Second World War was as a radar post but it was also a scrapyard for wrecked planes and a high explosive bomb dump. The land was returned to its original owners, the Wests, after the Second World War and much of the site remains poluuted by caustic soda, a by-product of hydrogen production.

Horsey Floods, 1938. The Norfolk coastline fights a constant and wearying battle against the sea. Millions of pounds have been invested in attempts to establish defences against this troublesome invader. On wild nights of high swelling seas the defences are at their most vulnerable. Freak waves or exceptional weather conditions cannot be predicted and the defences can be breached. On the night of 13 February 1938 the seas were whipped into a frenzy by a northerly gale which left a trail of destruction from The Wash to Southwold in Suffolk. Poor little Horsey was to receive the worst of it when a tidal wave smashed through the coastline for 700 yards causing the biggest coastal breach for fifty years. The true extent of such damages can best be observed from the air. The floods covered 15 square miles of farms and marshes. The village was surrounded by sea and its inhabitants had to be evacuated. The East Norfolk River Catchment Board, who originally commissioned these photos, assessed that the damage amounted to about £13,000 at Horsey alone.

Hethel aerodrome, 1948. Pictured while still occupied by the RAF, the airfield was begun in 1941 by George Wimpey & Co. Ltd and completed the following year. The first American unit to move in was the 320th Bombardment Group in November 1942. The base did not receive its principal fighting unit until June 1943 when the 389th Bombardment Group arrived. The first of over 300 operational missions flown from Hethel before the end of the war was undertaken on 7 September 1943. The Americans left in May 1945, the airfield passed to Fighter Command and Polish-manned Mustang squadrons moved in shortly after. The base was eventually transferred to Technical Training Command and was classed 'inactive' by 1948.

Lotus Cars Ltd, Hethel, 1970. The fate of the old flying base at Hethel was not to be that of so many old aerodromes, which are now overgrown and ruinous or ploughed up and back to farmland. The site was eventually sold in 1964 to Lotus Cars. The old hangars and workshops were used for the manufacture of the cars and 2.2 miles of the old runway was used as a test track. Now supplemented by a constantly growing number of new buildings, the new factory is actually located on the old airbase's technical site. All Lotus cars are still developed and produced exclusively at Hethel.

Haymaking, 1951. A familiar sight across the great agricultural fields of Norfolk, the harvest of barley is the finest in all England. These fields were the cradle of the Agrarian Revolution. Viscount 'Turnip' Townshend at Raynham and the Cokes half a century later at Holkham developed and popularised the pioneering work of their seventeenth-century predecessors. They introduced turnips and root crops to improve the quality and productivity of the land as part of the Norfolk four-course crop rotation (turnips, clover, barley, wheat). In addition, by turning the soil upside down and laying marl from underneath on top of the sandy soil, and by enclosing much of the land, they converted comparatively unproductive sheep walks into profitable wheatfields.

Farming methods have changed at an incredible pace over the last 100 years. Now fields may be harvested in hours rather than the days it once took. If only aerial photography had been around at the turn of the century to capture rows of scythemen mowing by hand, 'putting their backs into it', proceeding across the field in line, sweeping their well-honed blades in time with the old 'Lord of the Mow'. All were followed by carts, boys riding trace horses, ladies raking the hay and older farm workers pitching the stooks into the cart. Small children with sticks ran ahead catching rabbits, hares and mice as they ran out of the field – what a sight that must have been!

East Dereham nine-hole golf course, covering about 80 acres, 1960. It was opened in 1934 under the auspices of Major Henry Piers Clarke of Scarning. The course is bordered on the left by Sandy Lane, off which the Humbletoft housing estate now stands, and Quebec Road is to the right. The latter's course may be observed almost all the way to North Elmham on this photograph. To the upper right of centre may be seen Quebec House, which gives its name to the road. The mansion was built in the Gothic style at the time of the capture of Quebec by General James Wolfe in 1759. The trees in the grounds were planted in the formation of the troops at the battle. Today the house and adjoining buildings are Quebec Hall Christian Eventide Home.

The Royal Norfolk Show, 1955. Every June the smartly ordered lines of stands, marquees and swarms of visitors mark one, unique corner of the Norfolk countryside. An essential feature of county life since 1847, the Royal Norfolk Show was once itinerant and was held at locations including East Dereham, King's Lynn, Great Yarmouth, Harleston and Diss. In 1953 the Show was held for the first time on its own home ground, purchased by the Royal Norfolk Agricultural Association at Costessey. All subsequent shows have been held at the site, which has also hosted many other major local events.

New drainage system, south of Downham Market, 1964. The Great Ouse rises near Brackley, Northamptonshire, and after meeting the Little Ouse it crosses the west end of Norfolk to Lynn, where is is joined by the Nar from the east. It then pursues its northward course to the sea nearly 60 miles away. It has been an important trade route in and out of Norfolk since ancient times. In the mid-nineteenth century it was navigable for barges 24 miles above Lynn and for smaller boats as far as Bedford, forming a link through other rivers to the Midlands. Much of the land along its length has always suffered a serious threat that has had to be constantly checked – flooding. Channels to help combat this have been cut along the Ouse since the thirteenth century. Vermuyden tackled this problem with his operations in the seventeenth century and it was addressed again in the nineteenth century with the construction of the Eau Brink Cut and work of the Norfolk Estuary Company. By 1900 Hunt's Sluice and the pumping station at Ten Mile Bank were responsible for the drainage of 30,000 acres, emptying fen water into the Ouse at the rate of 130 tons a minute. After the construction of Denver Sluice, in connection with the Hundred Feet River, an additional 800,000 acres of land now have their flood waters carried off. Following the horrific floods of 1937, 1947 and 1953 major works had to be carried out to address this old problem again, and new cuts were made under a new scheme including the non-navigable Cut Off Channel skirting the fens. This carries excess water from the upper reaches of the eastern tributaries to the Relief Channel, near Denver Sluice, which was completed in 1964.

Bacton Gas Terminal, 1972. Development of this site was initiated in 1967 and it began receiving gas in 1968. Considerable investment, constant development and refinement have altered the site. The terminal today consists of three separate facilities operated by Shell, BP Amoco and Phillips. In addition, TransCo has a plant which receives the treated gas.

The site's function is to separate the condensate liquids from the incoming gas stream, separate out the heavier, lower boiling point fractions by cooling (using a propane refrigeration plant), rewarming and finally filtering before metering out to TransCo. Separate condensate liquids are transported through a 6 inch pipeline to the rail terminal at North Walsham from where they are transported for use as refinery feed stock.

The latest project involving the terminal follows its selection as the landing location for SEAL (Shearwater and Elgin Area Line), which will be the first where gas from the central North Sea has been shipped directly to the Bacton Gas hub.

Norwich

Norwich, 1920. How appropriate that the earliest Norwich photograph from the Aerofilms archive should centre on the castle, the city's first major building. Begun in 1068, two years after the Norman Conquest, as an earthwork and timber fortification, it was faced with stone, about 1120. The royal castle – the only one of its kind in Norfolk and Suffolk – was held by a Constable for the King. In 1220 the castle became the county gaol. Between 1824 and 1839 it was greatly enlarged and wings were added to the old stone keep to house 224 male prisoners. At the bottom of the slope are the Castle Ditches. Gallows would be constructed between the two small gatehouses so that the assembled masses could view the execution of criminals, the last of which was carried out in 1867. The prison remained functional until August 1887 when the inmates were transferred to the gaol on Mousehold Heath. After a major conversion costing £22,474 the old keep and its annexes became the Castle Museum. Opened on 23 October 1894, it is still going strong today as a museum and headquarters of the Norfolk Museums Service.

The full extent of the Cattle Market may also be observed. Its pens extended to the Agricultural Hall (middle right). The market on this land could be traced back to the twelfth century. By the twentieth century the 8½ acre site hosted 6 firms of auctioneers and 33 private dealers selling 212,000 head of stock and 100,000 head of fowl and turkey per annum. The cattle market was moved to its Hall Road site in 1960. This site, after a few years as a car park, has now been completely redeveloped as the Castle Mall shopping complex.

Norwich, August 1926. Here we view the city from the river. Running diagonally along the lower half of the photograph is King Street, one of the most historic streets in the city. A pathway has existed here since Roman times. The Saxons made their first settlement in the area beside the river and just beyond the King's Ford (Conesford). King's Street was a collection of fashionable houses from Jacobean times, but by the nineteenth century the situation had changed and it had become an industrial area surrounded by rows of workers' houses. Along the length of the road there were forty-three pubs and beerhouses at the beginning of the twentieth century. When this photograph was taken there were thirteen with three active breweries (Youngs, Crawshay & Youngs, Morgans and Whitbread) along its length. In fact breweries and factories may be identified by their chimneys all across the city on this photograph. Today there are very few old brick factory chimneys left standing in Norwich.

Norwich city centre, 1928. Along the lower foreground is Rampant Horse Street running into Theatre Street. The now demolished Presbyterian chapel is visible on the far left. Just below centre and to the right is the fluid curve of Orford Place round into Gentleman's Walk which passes through the centre of the photograph. Just beyond St Peter Mancroft church may be seen the old municipal buildings and market stalls; this area, along with St Peter's Street immediately behind, was demolished in 1937 to make way for the new City Hall and Market. Follow the line of Gentleman's Walk down to the bottom of Exchange Street: opposite this junction stands the grand structure that was F.W. Harmer & Co., Manufacturing Clothiers. The company, founded in 1826, had its St Andrew's steam clothing and hosiery works here. Harmer's won government contracts to make uniforms and the factory was hit several times during the blitz until it was finally burnt to the ground by fire bombs in 1943. Harmer's found alternative premises and carried on its business. Today most of the old factory site is taken up by the St Andrew's car park.

Works of A.J. Caley & Son Ltd, 1928. Mr A.J. Caley came to Norwich to establish his chemist's business on London Street in 1857. In 1863 he began producing a mineral water in his cellar, and pleasantly surprised at its popularity he soon moved to a large premises on Bedford Street. He was joined in the business in 1878 by his son Edward J. Caley and they moved to even larger premises on Chapel Field where they produced a wide variety of drinks from soda and seltzer to lemonade and their famous ginger ale. In 1883 they started manufacturing cocoa and then chocolate in 1886. The business went from strength to strength and a new factory was erected where they began to make Christmas crackers. They were soon to be sending exports all over the world and enjoying royal patronage. The business remained in Caley family hands until 1918 when it was bought by the African & Eastern Trading Corporation who sold it to John Mackintosh & Sons in 1932. This factory was totally burnt out by incendiary bombs in 1942 but was rebuilt in 1946: the smell of warm chocolate from the new factory filled the city air again. It was taken over by Nestlé in the 1980s but the factory buildings now face an uncertain future after their final closure in 1997. As a footnote, the Caley brand name was purchased by some of the managers of the closing factory and Caley's Marching Chocolate is now being made in Norwich again.

Boulton & Paul's Riverside Works, 1928. When William Staples Boulton joined Joseph John Paul in a growing engineering, ironmongery and agricultural equipment manufacturing business in 1868, I wonder whether they had any idea that they would become one of the most famous business partnerships in the history of the city? Initial investment was put into new wire netting manufacturing machines and developing a range of steel- and timber-framed buildings for both industrial and domestic use. Boulton & Paul soon became world famous. In 1915 the company began another chapter in its illustrious history when it was asked to produce aircraft for the war effort. It completed 2,530 planes by the end of the war. By the time this photograph was taken the firm had developed the first twin-engined, all metal, biplane bomber – the Sidestrand. It was also here that framework for airship *R101* was constructed. Although the aircraft side of the business was sold off in the 1930s the Riverside works developed and during the Second World War handled contracts for items as diverse as Morrison shelters and noses for Horsa gliders. After a number of take-overs beginning in the 1960s the business sadly declined and many long-serving staff were made redundant. The Riverside Works have recently been demolished to make way for the Riverside Development, and the name of Boulton & Paul tragically no longer appears among the trading businesses of Norwich.

The Norfolk & Norwich Hospital, 1928. A hospital was founded here in 1771 and was rebuilt on part of the original site in 1882. The first stone of the new building was laid by the Prince of Wales (later Edward VII) in June 1879. The buildings, built on the pavilion system in the form of a letter H, were designed by Norwich architects Messrs Boardman and Wyatt, and were opened fully furnished for the grand sum of £60,000. These old buildings, although they are covered by a preservation order, face an uncertain future as construction begins on the long discussed new Norfolk & Norwich hospital at Colney.

The first circle of houses, Mile Cross Corporation Housing Estate, Norwich, 1928. During the depressed interwar years Norwich authorities, mostly in an effort to find work for the many returned servicemen, set about a sweeping development programme of parkland construction and council housing estates – the first scheme of its kind in the country. About 5,000 houses were built on a total of six estates on the outskirts of the city and the first house was let in October 1920. When this photograph was taken houses were let for the net rent of 5s, with 3d rates, 7d electricity assessment charge and, in some cases, additional charges of 6d for hot water and 2½d for electric current.

Bishop Bridge Gas Works, 1932. In 1815 John Taylor, a Norwich inventor, obtained a patent for apparatus to assist in the decomposition of certain animal substances, including oil, from which he discovered he could procure gas 'useful as an illuminant'. Taylor, with his partner Martineau, exhibited the appliance at Apothecaries' Hall in 1819 and the following year they formed the Norwich Gas Company. They obtained parliamentary authority for the laying of pipes for public supply and a gas works, powered by oil, was built on St Stephen's Back Street. They sold it to the British Gas Light Company in 1825, which built this coal gas works near Bishop Bridge for the grand sum of £40,000.

St Martin-at-Palace Gas Works, 1932. Demand for gas supply grew; by the middle of the nineteenth century many of the city streets were lit by gas and the number of households using gas for lighting and domestic purposes was growing rapidly. The Bishop Bridge works were extended and a new gas holder was erected, leaving very little available space on the site for further development. Land was purchased a little further away at St Martin-at-Palace and a new works was constructed between 1851 and 1853. Between 1920 and 1922 these works were extended to include further retort houses and a carburetted water gas plant at a cost of £236,000. The two gas works supplied most of the city of Norwich under the control of the British Gas Light Company for well over 100 years until they were brought into public ownership with the creation of the Eastern Gas Board in 1949. In the 1960s natural North Sea gas was discovered as a cheaper alternative to the manufacturing plants, Bacton Gas terminal was begun and the old works in the city and across Norfolk were closed, demolished and gasometers taken down (with the exception of Fakenham, which is now a museum). The site of the Palace Gas Works is now occupied by the city's new law courts and all that remains of Bishop Bridge works is the skeleton of one of its gas holders, a remnant of industrial archaeology and a familiar part of the city skyline.

The Firs Racetrack photographed in 1932, shortly after its official opening. The track began life as a venue for dog racing and was occasionally used for miniature car races and motorcyle speedway. By the mid-1930s The Boundary had become the city's main dog racing track and The Firs was dedicated to speedway. It had been bought up by Max Crosskeuts, not only a rider himself but also a designer and promoter. He built up the terrace on the bends with railway sleepers and laid a good cinder track. Racing stopped through the war years as the floodlights could not be used because of blackout restrictions. After the war The Firs enjoyed its golden years with names like Billy Bales, Phil Clarke, Paddy Mills, Peter Craven, Aub Lawson and Ove Fundin, to name but a few. The venue achieved national fame. In 1964 the axe fell on The Firs when the speedway track was sold for about £75,000 to become a housing estate, bringing to an end Norwich Motorcycle Speedway.

Eaton Park, 1932. In 1906 the city authorities bought 80 acres of arable land and fields from the Church Commissioners. For eighteen years after it was acquired Eaton Park remained a simple grassy enclosure where occasional fairs and shows were held. Shortly after the First World War, there were many unemployed men in the city. To find them work a scheme was devised to lay out Eaton Park as formal gardens. The plan, drawn up by Captain Sandys Winch, Superintendent of the Parks and Gardens, was approved in 1924. For the next three-and-a-half years two-thirds of Eaton Park was developed, providing labour for 103 unemployed men a week. In the middle of the park the fine colonnaded circle was constructed with the bandstand in the centre. Mr A.E. Collins, the City Engineer, designed the model yacht pond and lily pond whose construction took eighteen months, providing work for fifty men a week. By 1928 the work was completed and in May the Duke of Windsor officially opened the park. It was a remarkable achievement with 6 full-size bowling greens, 35 grass tennis courts, 12 hard tennis courts, 10 cricket pitches, 5 hockey pitches and 14 football pitches. As many as 600 people could take part in organised games here at any one time.

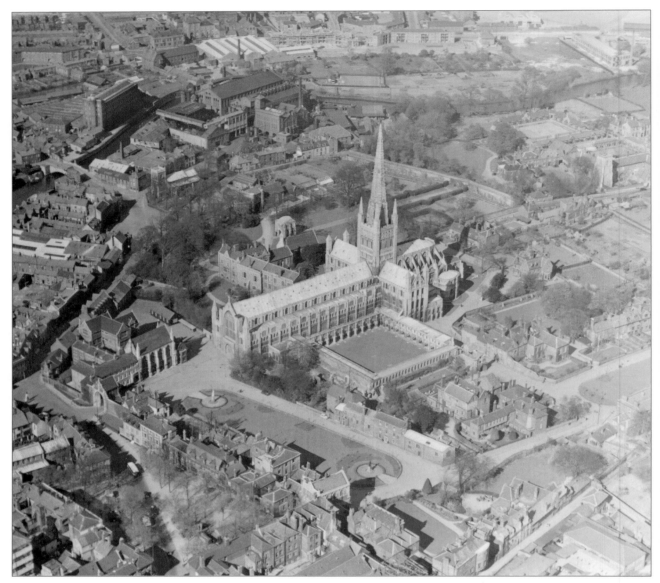

Norwich Cathedral, 1939. Viewed from the Upper Cathedral Close, across Almary Green, is the outstanding, lofty Norman edifice of Norwich Cathedral. It was begun in 1096 by Bishop Herbert de Losinga shortly after he moved the seat of the Bishopric to the city from Thetford. Sadly he was not to see his new building finished; his successor Eborard completed the church by about 1140. The cloisters and monastic precincts adjoining the cathedral were severely damaged during a riot in 1272. So fierce was the fighting it took a King's army to restore order. The people of Norwich were fined as a consequence and the new Ethelbert Gate was built as a further 'penance'. The original spire, constructed from wood, was destroyed in the hurricane of 1362. It was replaced by the 315 foot stone spire we know today, which was completed in 1480. This picture was taken on the eve of the Second World War but little has changed in the cathedral precincts to this day. It survived the firebomb blitz of 1942 with superficial damage to a transept roof. Sadly the rest of the city did not fare so well.

Norwich, 1946. The view from St Stephen's Street on to Surrey Street and Westlegate. This area was subject to some of the worst damage inflicted on the city by air raids during the Second World War, particularly during the 'Baedeker blitz' a period of bombing believed to have been planned around the famous Baedeker travel guides when Hitler specifically targeted cities of great historical interest in an attempt to break morale) in 1942. The famous thatched Boars Head pub, which once stood on the corner of Surrey Street and St Stephen's, was burnt out by fire bombs. The next bomb site in the middle distance was the site of Bond's department store, destroyed during the same raid.

The heart of Norwich, 1946. By the grace of God it was not reduced to rubble like so many other city centres across the country. In relation to the damage that did occur here, people applied the wartime maxim of 'make do and mend' and carried on as best they could. Standing proud in the middle of the picture, with its sand-bags recently removed, is the City Hall. This classic 1930s municipal building, designed by C.H. James and S.R. Pierce, was rather cruelly described by a contemporary as 'resembling a marmalade factory'. The building, along with the new Italian paved marketplace, was opened with much civic pomp on 29 October 1938. To the middle right of the picture is another landmark sadly now lost – the Corn Exchange, on Exchange Street. The original Corn Hall was built in 1826 and then replaced by this larger building in 1861. Here agricultural trading, exhibitions, boxing matches and entertainments were held until it was demolished in 1963.

Prefabricated estate, Norwich, 1946. So many people were bombed out of their homes during the Second World War that there was a desperate need for emergency housing after 1945. Out of this need was born the 'pre-fab', and here we see Norwich's first effort at a pre-fab estate. The area where it was built has a chequered past. It was once all part of Mousehold Heath but was not included in the designated area of the heath preserved under order as a public open space in 1884. The land was then taken over in 1914 by the Royal Flying Corps as an airfield, passing in 1927 to the Norfolk and Norwich Aero Club. In 1933 it was officially opened as the Norwich Municipal Aerodrome. During the Second World War it was a decoy airfield, becoming a prefab estate in 1946. All that was left of the airfield was a helicopter airmail base, which was closed in the 1960s. As the airport receded the other land off Plumstead Road was acquired by builders, and a new estate began to emerge. It was extensively developed in the 1960s. The estate and general area are now known as the Heartsease.

Norwich, 1949. The city is viewed from the north-west, Heigham Street area. Cutting away from the bottom left are the sidings and buildings of the Norwich City station. It was opened by the Eastern and Midlands Railway Company in 1882 for passenger, general goods and livestock traffic. In 1893 the line was taken over by the Midland and Great Northern Railway and extensive sidings and warehouses were erected. By the 1930s about one-third of railborne goods traffic for Norwich was dealt with at this station. Wrecked during the blitz of 1942, the station buildings we see here are prefabricated. Ten years later in February 1959, along with the rest of the M&GN, the station closed to passengers. Although it ran freight for a few years after the station closure, the site was totally demolished and cleared in 1971. All traces of the railway have now disappeared beneath an industrial estate and the Norwich inner ring road.

Norwich City Corporation Electricity Power Station, Crown Point, 1951. The first electricity power supply to the city was established by a private company in 1893. The operation was taken over by the City Corporation in 1902 and a generating station was situated on Duke Street. By 1924 demand was surpassing output. As a result land was purchased at Crown Point by the River Wensum and a new power station was opened in 1926 at a cost of £289,000 with a further extension in 1929 for £100,000. By this time over 80 miles of high-tension main, mostly overhead, had been carried out to the surrounding towns. In 1935 over 39,000 domestic premises in the area had been connected to electricity. The Eastern Electricity Board took over the operation in the 1960s, and although the power station was modernised and extended it was eventually demolished and replaced by another plant on the same site. This has recently been closed down.

Norwich, 1957. The city centre was still undergoing change as a result of postwar development. New factories and shops were built to replace those destroyed in the blitz. Just a casual glance at the published Norwich City Plan of 1945 horrifies the viewer – in fact the developers planned to destroy more of the historic city centre than the Luftwaffe ever did. The sweeping and drastic plans were supposed to transform the city centre into open shopping 'plains', removing row upon row of classic historic buildings by architects like George Skipper in favour of typical 1950s shopping precinct-style premises. Fortunately, the plans were not implemented in their entirety. A hint of what the city could have looked like if the development had not taken place may be derived from the example in the centre of this picture. The small cluster of streets around Lady Lane and Bethel Street were demolished to make way for the Norwich Central Library and car park, opened in 1963. There was a terrible fire in the library in 1994 and the loss of historic books was mourned. The loss of the building is, however, far less lamented and we hope its replacement will have a more timeless appeal.

Norwich City FC football ground, 1961. Having played in its early days on the old Corporation football ground on Newmarket Road, Norwich City FC moved to its first purpose-built ground, The Nest on Rosary Road, in 1907. In 1934 the Football Association informed Norwich City that The Nest was inadequate for second division football. A new site was found on Carrow Road. Using some of the old materials from The Nest (conveyed to the new site by horse and cart) the new stands were built by Boulton & Paul, financed mostly by the City's Vice President Captain Evelyn Barclay. The City's new ground was opened on 31 August 1935 by the Lord Lieutenant of Norfolk, Mr Russell Colman.

This photograph shows the ground in 1961 shortly after its purchase from Boulton & Paul for £60,000. (It had been rented from the company since 1935.) We can also see the South Stand with its new roof – seats followed in the 1970s. The River End's roofed stand was constructed in 1979. The City stand suffered a fire in 1984, but was rebuilt by 1986. In 1992, in the wake of the Hillsborough disaster, the Barclay Stand was demolished, rebuilt and fitted with seats and thus Norwich City became an all-seater stadium. Today the ground, which can seat a capacity crowd of almost 22,000, is estimated to be worth about £25 million.

Thorpe station (photographed 1968) was built by Young & Son for £60,000 and opened in May 1886. Today Thorpe is the city's only surviving operative station serving both passengers and goods traffic. Through this station came many of the great names of the golden age of steam, including 'The Broadsman', 'The Norfolkman' and 'The East Anglian'. During the early 1950s the station annually issued 500,000 tickets and 20,000 seat reservations. This view shows the station just over ten years after the first electric train made the run from Norwich to London and diesel railcars were then becoming a familiar sight on the local services.

Throughout the 1980s and '90s the station underwent constant change. In the mid-'80s a new goods depot was built at Crown Point and new track layout and signalling have been installed. Following privatisation (and with ongoing support from Railtrack) the Norwich terminal underwent a £3 million structural restoration in 1997/98. An interior renovation project is due for completion by 2000. Well over 1 million passengers now pass through Thorpe station every year.

In the bottom right of the photograph is Laurence, Scott & Electromotors Ltd's Gothic Works on Hardy Road, constructed in 1896. Laurence & Scott has been associated with Norwich for well over 100 years. Although the company was sold to engineering giants FKI, it still trades on the same site under the same name and is one of the few Norwich businesses that still takes on apprentices.

An overview of the city of Norwich, 1969. George Borrow (1803–81), recalling his Norwich boyhood wrote, 'A fine old city, truly, is that, view it from what side you will; but it shows best from the east, where the ground, bold and heavy, overlooks the fair and fertile valley in which it stands. . .' I wonder what he would have said if he could have seen this view of his find city! He would naturally recognise the course of the River Wensum, the cathedral and castle but no doubt he would have been shocked by how much Norwich has grown since he knew it when the population numbered 36,909 and Norwich was still contained within the bounds of the medieval city wall. By 1969 many of the outlying villages known to Borrow, such as Drayton, Earlham, Catton and Costessey, have become suburbs of the city. So much has changed since even this photograph was taken. In 1969 the city still had its long-established, 'household name' businesses of shoe-making, mustard, brewing, engineering and chocolate. Today, the factories and breweries have been sold and/or moved out of the city centre. The works now stand redundant, have been demolished or converted to offices or flats. However, the outlook for the city is far from dismal. Large insurance companies and office-based industries have centres all over Norwich. New shops in the Castle Mall complement those already flourishing and indeed many of the old businesses have expanded over recent years (although, tragically we have lost a fair few along the way). The traditional businesses have recently begun anew making chocolate and brewing good local ales, albeit on a smaller scale. Remember, 'from tiny acorns. . .'

Norwich, 1972. Across the middle of this photograph we can trace the course of Magdalen Street on its final leg out of the city through the ruins of the Magdalen Gates opposite the Artichoke public house (far middle left). This land outside the city's ancient defensive walls was developed into terraced housing from old field land from the late 1870s. Although damaged during the blitz the area just within the walls could have been much restored to its early Victorian-fronted charm, fondly remembered for shops like Peacock's Bazaar Price Stores and the Elephant public house. Instead it was considered that an inner link road and shopping precinct would be preferred so the demolition teams waded in during the late 1960s, cutting a great swathe up to Magdalen Street then pushing the new roadway aloft right over the street with a hideous concrete flyover, its construction causing the demolition of the ancient area of Magdalen Street known as Stump Cross. The buildings in the centre from the Anglia Square shopping precinct, a multi-storey car park, cinema and office blocks occupied until recently by Her Majesty's Stationery Office (HMSO) and Central Computer and Telecommunications Agency (CCTA). Unbelievably the old HMSO building received a design award. The old CCTA building, Gildengate House, has been put to good use as it is the temporary home for the Norfolk Local Studies Library and the Norfolk Record Office while their new building is being erected.

County Towns & Villages

Gaymer's Cider Works, Attleborough, 1932. The business can trace its roots back to the 1700s and probably operated before that date at Banham, where generations of the Gaymer family produced cider to sell at The Crown, the inn they kept in the village. In the late nineteenth century the entreprenurial William Gaymer (1842–1936) began to take his cider to international exhibitions and won medals. Others began to appreciate this fine beverage and a demand for it grew. Larger purpose-built premises were constructed near the railway at Attleborough. By 1906 Gaymer's was a limited company, employing 400 men. It had a Royal Warrant, a contract with the House of Commons and a flourishing export trade all over the world. For generations the cider factory was Attleborough's largest employer and it contributed much to the fabric of the community. In 1961 the company was taken over by Showerings, the makers of Babycham. Showerings merged with Allied Lyons and in 1992 the Gaymer Group was sold for £140 million in a management buyout. Sadly the deal was not a great success and Matthew Clark, Britain's third biggest cider maker, bought the group for £109 million. The new owners shut the plant within weeks of closing the deal in October 1994, by this one act bringing to an end 200 years of Norfolk cider making by Gaymer's.

Attleborough, 1932. When this photograph was taken the town numbered 2,608 souls, the streets were lit by gas lamps and domestic electricity was supplied by the Norwich City Corporation. The town is, in fact, ancient. It is recorded in Domesday as Attelbure and John Brame, the historian monk of Thetford, claimed it was founded by Atlinge, the then King of the province, to oppose Rond, the King of Thetford. Attleborough is said to have grown to be one of the largest settlement towns in Norfolk. The early importance of the town, although lost after the Norman Conquest, was still reflected for many years in the markets and annual fairs held within its bounds. Up to the nineteenth century a grand fortnightly trading and livestock market was held in addition to a small weekly market, which was held on Fridays. Three annual fairs were held, one each on the Thursdays before Easter Sunday and Whit Sunday, and one on 15 August for 'cattle and pedlary'. A fourth 'pleasure' fair was held on the last day before the March assizes. This latter fair originated from the throngs who flocked to the town to see the prisoners pass *en route* from Thetford to Norwich. Visitors were certainly able to travel to and from the town in style after the granting of the 1695 Turnpike Act; one of the very first of such road improvement schemes in the county, the road initially linked Wymondham and Attleborough. It was then extended to Newmarket in 1768, and it eventually enabled the first maintained link road to be created from Norfolk to London.

Aylsham, 1932. At this time the population of 2,646 had their homes lit by gas supplied by the Aylsham Gas Light Co. There was no direct electricitiy supply, no piped domestic sewerage system and no water supply except from wells. The town is in countryside once known as 'The Garden of Norfolk'. In this picture we see an evocative image of horse and cart crossing the marketplace towards the old North Norfolk Supply Stores. In Domesday Aylsham's Manor is recorded as extending to Tuttington, including Dunkirk and Drabblegate, and had '18 carucates, 20 villeins and 28 bordars with woods enough for the maintenance of 400 swine'. Its market can be traced back to the thirteenth century, and was famed in the fourteenth century for its linen known as 'Aylsham Webbs'. This trade was replaced by the great popularity during Tudor and Stuart times of the framework knitting of worsted stockings, breeches and waistcoats. Dominating this view, taken from the north-west, is St Michael's church built by John of Gaunt, Duke of Lancaster, after the manor was granted to him in 1372 by his father Edward III. A notable monument in the churchyard by the south wall of the chancel is the tomb of Humphrey Repton, the great eighteenth-century landscape gardener. Aylsham was one of the county's spa towns during the eighteenth century. The spa or 'spaw' was located about half a mile from the town. A chalybeate spring full of iron salts, owned in latter years by a Mr Elvin, was 'much resorted to by invalids afflicted by asthma and other chronic diseases'.

Aylsham, 1953. We view the town from the Marsham side before there were major residential developments beyond the cemetery and water tower. At the time this photograph was taken there were 775 inhabited houses and a total of 2,526 registered residents in the town. The focus of Aylsham's civic and one-time merchant centre is the Town Hall seen facing us to the right of the marketplace. It was built as a Town Hall and Corn Hall in 1857 for £2,100, funded by the issue of £10 shares. It was extended in 1892, and was acquired by the parish council in September 1908 after a loan was agreed from Norfolk County Council. A total of £1,400 was borrowed (£1,200 for purchase and £200 for renovation). The loan was repaid by 1931 and the parish council undertook the running of the Town Hall as a non-profit-making concern. Events, entertainments, public meetings and all manner of town engagements are still held in the grand old hall to this day.

Besthorpe, 1973. All around this village may be found ancient moated sites, remnants of past inhabitants great and humble, who benefited from the area's rich soil and abundance of wood. The great have certainly been associated with the village and the manors of the Plasset, Bavent, Page, and Brettenham families all fall within the parish. Besthorpe Hall itself was built by Sir William Drury in 1590 and has connections with the Needhams, Earls and Viscounts Kilmorey; a tilting ground was maintained at the hall until the nineteenth century. Pictured here before the construction of the Wymondham bypass, Besthorpe had already been cut in two by the busy A11. In fact this road was the first highway of its kind in the country as it was the first turnpike route set up by the Government Act in 1695. It became part of the first link road between Norwich and London.

Burnham Market, 1951. Now including the parishes of Burnham Sutton, Burnham Ulph and Burnham Westgate, Burnham Market is chief of the seven Burnhams. Most of the field land directly in front of the church has now been developed as residential housing. The long green, surrounded by beautiful Georgian-fronted buildings and triangulated by the town's roadways, was once occupied by a fortnightly market. Just off the green is the white frontage of The Hoste Arms Hotel. The building dates back to 1550 and has been used as a hotel since the late seventeenth century. In 1999 it was voted the second favourite hotel in England in a poll by *The Times* and twenty-seventh favourite in the world.

Clenchwarton, 1971. Its name means 'sluice-guarding town' and it was once divided into two, North and South Clenchwarton. Set on a peninsula almost surrounded by navigable rivers and an arm of the sea, the salt marshes of this parish extend to The Wash between Terrington and North Lynn. The area is well intersected with drains and ditches to draw off the waters. In the early nineteenth century it was reckoned that no fewer than 111 bridges were to be found in this area. Despite being surrounded by washlands, the drinking water supply in the town was very poor and well into the twentieth century locals collected rain water in cisterns and boiled it before consumption. Land around the village, amounting to over 150 acres, was successfully reclaimed in the 1850s from the bed of the River Ouse under the auspices of the Eau Brink Commissioners.

Diss, 1964. Surrounded by gently undulating countryside towards the Norfolk and Suffolk border, Diss nestles around its Great Mere. The town was one of the first in the county to be illuminated by gas (from the works on Victoria Road built in 1835) and electricity (supplied by the East Anglian Electricity Supply Co. of Stowmarket). The Mere, around which the town has grown, acted as the town drain until the nineteenth century. It was, however, renowned for being well stocked with eels and a rare fish known as a 'chaser'. The old mere has served the town well over the years especially in 1640 when its plentiful water supply quenched the fire which threatened to engulf Diss. The town itself was built up around the triangular market-place. It is compact, with its 1854 corn exchange and magnificent clerestoried church all in close proximity. The toll-free Friday market in the nineteenth century included brisk trade in corn, cattle, sheep and pigs. Important stock sales were held weekly in the Saracen's Head Yard and by The Crown Hotel. An ancient sheep fair was also held twice a year; one on the last Thursday in June for lambs and the other on the second Thursday in August for ewes and rams.

Downham Market, 1928. The population when this picture was taken numbered 2,465. Downham was recorded as Duneham in Domesday and has market rights conferred by Edward the Confessor (*c.* 1003–66). The old Manor along with Clackclose hundred, in which the town stands, was given by King Edgar to Ramsey Abbey and by the time of Henry III (1216–72) the incumbent Abbot was invested with the right to try and execute malfactors at 'his gallows at Downham'. The town had an extensive butter market, held fortnightly every Monday, where in the height of summer and spring about 90,000 firkins were bought annually by factors, and sent to London to be sold under the name Cambridge Butter. In the modern market-place, just off centre of the photograph, is the distinctive clock tower built in the Gothic style from designs by William Cunliffe and presented to Downham in 1878.

St Nicholas' church, East Dereham, 1920. The church was founded along with a nunnery by St Withberga in the seventh century. Both were, however, tragically destroyed by Danish raiders. Such was the fame of Withberga's piety that pilgrims came here for many years after her death in 654. Buildings sprang up for their accommodation and supply of provisions – and in this way the foundations of Dereham town were laid out.

In the tenth century St Withberga's body was stolen by the jealous abbot and monks of Ely who buried her in their cathedral. Folklore tells that a spring gushed from her empty grave. Today St Withberga's well may be seen in a small vaulted chamber near the church. A second church was built by the Normans but the one we see today is predominantly Early English. Alterations began with the fall of the original bell tower in the early fourteenth century. A lantern tower was erected in the middle of the church to the west of the original. With the craftsmen 'on site', the opportunities for change and improvement were too good to miss, so pious local worthies took the chance to enlarge their church. Successive alterations and improvements, such as the construction of the Thomas à Becket and John the Baptist chapels, were carried out throughout the fourteenth century. A new bell tower was erected, detached from the church, in the early sixteenth century. It has a great clock and fine ring of eight bells. In 1796 it was used for the incarceration of French prisoners of war. After escaping from the tower, one of the prisoners was shot while hiding in a tree and is buried in the churchyard near where he fell. The magnificent church and the Bishop Bonner Cottages Museum (open through the summer months) are well worth a visit.

East Dereham, 1937. At the time the ecclesiastical parish was home to 5,794 people. The town in 'The Heart of Norfolk' had gas street lighting in 1937 supplied from the works on Yaxham Road and electricity was controlled by the local council. East Dereham had an excellent sewerage and drainage system. Its waterworks was erected in 1881 and the water supply derived from a deep well sunk at a cost of £4,000. The earliest account of the town comes from the age of the Saxon kings when Withberga, daughter of Anna, King of East Anglia, settled here about AD 650 and set up a nunnery. The town has been ravaged by fire twice. The first blaze was in July 1581 after which the marketplace was laid out in much the same form as we know it today. But then most of the rebuilt houses were destroyed in the second great fire in July 1670. Sadly, the reconstructed town was regarded as probably 'the dirtiest town in the county; the streets uneven and choked with filth' with certain lanes 'so narrow as to scarcely admit the passing of a carriage'. A resolution, greatly supported by the statesman and Norfolk landowner Sir Robert Walpole, was made in the 1730s to improve the situation by public subscription. The streets were levelled, paved and drained. The town was thus transformed and was described by William White in 1845 as 'one of the handsomest in the county . . . a spacious Market Place and several long streets lined with neat houses and well stocked shops'.

Emneth, 1962. In the early nineteenth century this hamlet was in the parish of Elm in Cambridgeshire but also being in the Freebridge Hundred of Norfolk it was always associated with the county and today is firmly on the Norfolk side of the border. Emneth is a beautifully situated village near the Smeeth on the east side of the River Nene. Blessed with richly fertile lands, it is surrounded by fruitful orchards and meadows. In 1933 there were over thirty-five fruit growers in the parish and the rich yields are a key feature of the rural economy even today.

Fakenham, 1928. The population at the time was 2,844, and their homes were lit by gas lamps supplied by the Fakenham Gas & Coke Co. Ltd, which was managed by William Lister. These Hempton Road works are today a museum of gas and local history. They are the oldest extant example of their kind in the country and were built in 1846. This picture was taken on one of the Thursday market days, the marketplace filled then as now by stalls of fruit, vegetables, provisions and housewares. Towards the top of the photograph is the Bridge Street cattle market, complete with its pens and stock. This was built in 1857. The stock sales held every Thursday from noon were presided over by Lond & Beck auctioneers. The town's oldest buildings date from the mid-eighteenth century and were constructed after a horrific fire engulfed many houses in 1738. Once a combined market cross and session house stood in the market-place. By ancient custom the inhabitants of the town were exempt from serving on juries outside of the parish. This right, along with the session house, passed into history when the sessions moved to Holt. The site was then marked at the turn of the nineteenth century with a pedestal and sun dial enclosed by iron palisades.

Fakenham School, 1928. Organised games in the schoolyard complete the scene at Fakenham's 'new' Public Elementary School on Queens Road. It was erected between 1912 and 1913, at a cost of £9,980, for 200 infants, 280 older boys and 270 older girls. This school replaced the four surviving mid-nineteenth-century schools built in the town, the oldest of these being the British School on Norwich Road, erected in 1844. The others were the National Boys' School on School Hill, erected in 1846, the National Girls' School on Wells Road (1848), and the National Infants' School on Wells Road (1848).

Feltwell, 1965. This is a large village on low fenland kept drained for many years by a 20hp steam engine erected in 1835. During the nineteenth century about thirty looms were active in the village weaving bombasine and crepes for the Norwich manufacturers. The village once had two churches. St Nicholas, the older, situated to the west of the village, was severely damaged by fire in 1494 and, although restored in the early nineteenth century, it fell into such disrepair that its chancel was pulled down in 1862 and its tower collapsed while being repaired in 1898. The second, adorned by a fine perpendicular tower, is St Mary's. With its stepped parapet and pinnacles it overlooks the whole village. The church itself was fully restored and enlarged during the 1860s.

Foulsham, 1968. A pretty Georgian village, its present structures mostly date from after June 1770 when the village was swept by a fire that consumed fourteen houses and reduced the church to a ruined shell. The damage amounted to a small fortune, but a collection was made and a play performed at Norwich for the 'benefit of sufferers' and the rebuilding began. The church of Holy Innocents with its 90 foot tower was completed in about 1489. It was restored after the 1770 fire, further renovation was undertaken in 1887 and completed in 1892, but then the great gale of 1895 caused yet further damage to the tower and church. It was restored again by the beginning of the twentieth century.

Harleston, 1964. The bend in the road just below centre of the photograph marks the junction of four streets and the site of the old marketplace. Once called Chapel Plain, the area was developed along with the site of the demolished chapel of ease (St John the Baptist) in 1873. The clock tower marks the spot of the old chapel and the cupola of the chapel is now fixed to the top of the tower. Almost directly behind the tower, on Broad Street, is the church of St John the Baptist, consecrated in June 1872. Also transferred to this new structure was the tradition begun in 1688 by Archbishop Sancroft, whereby an annuity was granted to the masters and fellows of Emmanuel College, Cambridge, to be paid to a clergyman, appointed by them, who should perform divine service in this chapel and teach a local school.

Hingham, 1963. A well-built town with two greens, it originally had a Saturday market, which was transferred in the nineteenth century to Tuesdays when corn and livestock sales were held at the Cock and Ringers Inns. The church of St Andrew, approached by an avenue of cyprus and yew, was built between 1316 and 1359 by its rector Remigius de Hethersete to replace its Norman predecessor. Although restored in the 1870s and '80s its appearance today would not be unfamiliar to the parents of Samuel Lincoln, who was baptised here in 1622. He set out for the New World in 1638 and his great-great-great-great grandson was Abraham Lincoln, President of the United States of America. Other founding fathers of America who came from the area gave Hingham, Massachusetts, its name. The link between the two communities has been strengthened by visits over the years.

Hockwold cum Wilton, 1965. This area was heavily settled in prehistoric times and the village is surrounded by sites of early habitation, round barrows and a 'ring ditch', remnants of great Bronze Age memorials. The united villages rest on the lower edge of fen country on the north vale of the Little Ouse river. In 1826 a suspension bridge was erected and a new improved road was laid across the river to Lakenheath in Suffolk. This river-crossing marked the boundaries of Norfolk and Suffolk but because of the alteration of the river's bed and changes in political boundaries it no longer accurately defines the county limits. There was once a village fair held here on St James' Day (25 July); originally the 'Wake of Wilton Church', it became known as Hockwold Fair for toys, peddlery and amusement and was held on the green around the ancient stone cross. The date of the fair was changed during this century to August Bank Holiday.

Ingoldisthorpe, 1971. Situated on the fringes of the Sandringham Estate, Ingoldisthorpe is seated in a picturesque valley full of cedars and oak. It is watered by a small rivulet which flows westward across the salt marshes to The Wash. People have obviously loved this little village over the years; it is well kept and has a charity established by Agnes Bigge in the sixteenth century and maintained to this day.

In the centre of the photograph is the church of St Michael, which houses a number of notable memorials. One of them commemorates Richard Gardiner who died after a short residence at Mount Amelia (Ingoldisthorpe Hall) in 1781. He was a busy partisan during election times and left behind him a great variety of *jeu d'esprit* songs and inscriptions full of wit and humour. Arthur Mee said of him: 'He was a gifted, lively and malicious mischief-maker whose writings under the name of "Dick Merryfellow" gave much offence.'

Loddon, 1928. The town, at the time, was home to 1,019 souls. All water was still supplied from wells. The town is made distinctive by its single long street, across which many good seventeenth- and eighteenth-century houses face each other, and its spacious market-place. It is still home to a market which can trace its charters back to Edward I (1272–1307) although it is greatly diminished in size from the days when there was a market every Tuesday for corn and Messrs Waters & Son had stock sales on alternate Mondays at the rear of the Swan Inn. The chapel of St Mary was replaced by the perpendicular church of the Holy Trinity, built in the fifteenth century by Sir James Hobart. A number of his family's memorials appear therein, including one to Lady Dionis Williamson (died 1684), the biggest contributor to the rebuilding of St Paul's Cathedral; she gave £2,000.

North Walsham, 1928. The grand old parish church of St Nicholas with its distinctive ruined tower is situated near the market-place. It marks the centre of the town in every way. The shape of the town as we see it dates from the great fire of North Walsham in 1600. In the foreground, behind its' tennis courted front lawn, is the Paston Grammar School (today the Paston Sixth Form). The original school was built by Sir William Paston as a free school in 1606 on land cleared by the great fire. To the right of the Grammar School lawn is one of the many lost and lamented buildings which once graced the town, the Corn Hall built in 1848 for £900. Having also served the town as its drill hall and centre for entertainments from boxing to dance nights, it was eventually sold to become an engineering works. Today the site is a car park.

North Walsham, 1973. Many changes have taken place in the town since even this picture was taken. Just below centre of this picture the open plain and stalls of the redundant cattle market can be seen. This site is now occupied by a supermarket. To the right of the church – commencing at the three-storey flats and descending towards the gasometers – are a car park, shopping precinct and close of houses built on the historic Dog Yard, Vicarage Street, Back Street and Ship Yard area of the town, demolished in the name of 'progress' in the late 1950s and early 1960s. The gasometers, a familiar part of the town skyline since the nineteenth century, also disappeared shortly after this photograph was taken.

Paston, 1969. Here was the home of the Paston family, made famous by their fifteenth-century family letters. Their great house stood just between St Margaret's church (where a number of the Paston family are laid to rest) and the only building left standing of the Paston's once sizeable estate – the Great Barn (above the church in this picture). Built by Sir William Paston in 1581 it is 164 feet long and is one of the largest in the county. Its brick and stone walls (probably from the ruins of Bromholm Priory) are capped with thatch. The barn was not only constructed as a store for the produce of the farm, it also stood as a status symbol and was used for village entertainments. The three offshoots of the long cattle shed and square fodder room are later additions. Today the barn is undergoing considerable restoration.

Reepham, 1968. Historically the town extended into the four parishes of Reepham St Mary, Kerdiston, Hackford and Whitwell. The market-place, central to the town, was all in Hackford parish. Market day was Wednesday and the town hosted a significant county market up the beginning of the twentieth century. There was a brisk trade in the rich barley grown in the region around the town and in the stock sale conducted by Messrs Ireland. Three churches stand in one churchyard. Two are roughly end to end and joined together – Whitwell church with its perpendicular tower, stands nearest the market-place while Reepham's tower stands to the south in the centre of the aisle. The third church, that of Hackford, stands aside and separate – in the ruined state it has been left in since it was burnt down with part of the town in 1500.

The developing housing estates at Roydon, 1973. In the top left of the photograph is the Perpendicular-style church of St Remigius. It is hard to imagine this area as open fields or to believe that in 1893 across these fields and along the lane opposite the church mustered the local rioters to protest against the proposed enclosure of common land on Brewer's Green by the Lord of the Manor. A series of protests culminated on 7 September, the night of the school board elections, when the land agent for the hall stood for election. Sensing hostility he stood down, but the villagers' blood was up and they threatened to burn an effigy of the agent to demonstrate their displeasure. The police had been forewarned and prevented this protest but the rioters became even more inflamed, tore the image to pieces, and stormed to Snow Street and the home of the agent. The police managed to hold them off through sallies of stones, the crowd eventually dispersed and eight of the 'ringleaders' were arrested the following day. The riots received national attention, and maybe had some influence on the Act approved later that year which forbade the enclosure of commons except with the approval of the Board of Agriculture.

Shelfanger, 1973. This area has long been renowned for the quality of its water and proliferation of wells. The earliest recorded in the area was noted by Blomefield as being a subterranean water conduit or mineral bath at Boyland Manor, constructed in the thirteenth century by Richard de Boyland.

In the 1870s when there was still a great vogue for taking waters two valuable mineral springs were developed from wells sunk at Hill House by its owner Dr Antony Charles Farringdon. He set up a spa house where he carbonated and bottled the water under trademark as 'Shelfanger Constitutional Waters'. By the early 1880s the approved waters led to the spa house being enlarged and a drinking fountain being installed, along with a plunge bath and other activities to promote health. By the beginning of the twentieth century competition, bad fortune and changing tastes brought about the end of the Shelfanger Spa, and although the wells still flow today the memory of Shelfanger as a spa village is a distant one.

A hay stack fire catches the cameraman's eye at Shelton, 1949. Before farming processes changed, thatched hay stack and rick yards were common sights across farming Norfolk. Although there was always a minority of mischief makers and thoughtless folk who would disregard cigarettes and cause the stack to 'fly a'fire' the greatest threat to the hay crop was spontaneous combustion. Hay should not be damp when it is stacked as this can cause it to heat up to such an extent it chars or catches fire. Long iron hay rods which probed the core of the stack were often incorporated when it was built. These were periodically removed to test the temperature. If it were judged to be excessive, ventilation holes were cut or the whole stack was moved.

Snetterton, 1963. Snetterton Heath Air Base was constructed by Taylor-Woodrow Ltd in 1942 at a cost of £950,000. The main runway (which cuts diagonally across the airfield as we view it) was 2,000 yards long while the two auxiliary runways were 1,400 yards each. The total area of concrete laid in its construction was 530,000 square yards with storage facilities constructed for 144,000 gallons of fuel.

The first unit to be stationed here was 386th Bomb Group of the 8th Army Air Force, which arrived in early June 1943. Its stay was a short one; just a week later it was moved for operational purposes to Essex. On 13 June the 96th Bomb Group arrived with its B-17F Fortresses. It went on to fly over 300 missions from Snetterton, many of them transporting senior members of the American military, who had been to 3rd Division HQ at nearby Elveden Hall. The smaller site on the other side of the A11 was proposed as an auxiliary depot when it was announced that five groups of B-24s were to be placed within the 3rd Air Division. Construction began in March 1944 and the Mobile Reclamation and Repair Squadron was transferred her from Necton. Work on this site, known as Eccles, ceased soon after conversion of the B-24 groups to B-17s was approved. The site was subsequently used for storage. Privately purchased after the war, Eccles is now an industrial engineering site.

Snetterton Heath airfield fell into disuse after the war and was privately purchased in 1952. The new owner turned the site into a motor racing circuit. The first race was held in 1953 and racing still carries on today, along with the further development of the site as the home of the Snetterton Sunday Market.

Stow Bardolph, 1972. This beautiful village is graced with the magnificent carstone church of Holy Trinity built in the Decorated style. It had fallen into a dilapidated state by 1779 and was rebuilt in 1796. It was rebuilt again in 1873 to the Tudor-style design of David Brandon. The village has been fortunate to have the caring patronage of the Hare family since 1553 when Sir Nicholas Hare bought the manor. His descendants have paid for church restorations, rebuilt the manor (twice), and built and endowed almshouses in the seventeenth century. In the church is the remarkable collection of Hare family memorials including the eerie life-size wax image of Sarah Hare. Contained in a mahogany cupboard, behind glass, she is dressed in the costume of 1744, the year she died. Another memorial worthy of note, placed there by Field Marshal Earl Roberts, is to James William Adams, Rector of Stow Bardolph 1895–1902, notable for being the first chaplain to receive the Victoria Cross. He won it during the Afghan War for rescuing men of the 9th Lancers who were pinned down, under fire and wounded in a stream at Killa Kazi on 11 December 1879.

Swaffham, 1928. The population at the time was 2,913 souls. The church of SS Peter and Paul, rebuilt in about 1454, proudly stands out from the lime trees, planted by William Fortin during the eighteenth century. Its tower and distinctive spire, the undoubted beacon of the town, are visible for miles around. An early, unplanned medieval town, Swaffham grew from the settlement around the important crossroads that had developed into the marketplace by the thirteenth century. A short distance from the church may be seen the handsome corn hall erected in 1858 for the grand sum of £1,800 raised in £5 shares. In the market-place, in the small triangular 'island', is the monument and drinking fountain erected by subscription in 1882 in honour of Sir William Bagge MP.

On Market Hill is the market cross, which consists of eight columns supporting a lead-covered dome crowned by the figure of Ceres, goddess of the harvest. This beautiful structure was erected by the Earl of Orford in 1783.

Terrington St Clement, 1930. The horticultural industry of the village can be seen in this photograph. The great diversity of crops grown across the 10,429 acres of marsh water and loamy soil in this parish included wheat, oats, potatoes, mustard seed, seed crops and sugar beet. Fruit and peas were grown for the local canning industry. The extensive glasshouses were used for flower and tomato growing. Over 100 acres were also dedicated to the cultivation of hyacinths and other bulbs.

Thetford, 1932. This was probably the most important of all the ancient market towns in Saxon and early Norman Norfolk with its castle, priory, cathedral and, at one time, twenty-four churches. It was the seat of the bishopric from 1075 to 1094, when Bishop Herbert de Losinga moved it to Norwich. Although time has not always been kind to the town it retains much of its rural charm. Sadly gone are the days of the four large fairs held in the town for sheep in May and August, for cattle and pedlary in September and for wool in August. There were even horse races held until the 1620s and revived again for a few years in the mid-nineteenth century. In the centre of the picture is the Guildhall where the quarter sessions for the borough were held. The original building on the site dated back to the fourteenth century. It was appointed the common hall of the corporation by Royal Charter in 1573. The old building was taken down and a new one was built in 1901 for £9,500.

Walpole St Peter with Walpole St Andrew in the background, 1969. Resting on the Norfolk and Cambridge borders surrounded by rich fen farmland are the Walpoles, which gave the name to the family that presented England with its first Prime Minister. The Walpole family lived here from the time of the Conquest and they left for Houghton, the village they are most often associated with, in the mid-thirteenth century. Centre stage of this picture, and justly so, is St Peter's church with its rows of thirteen clerestory windows, plus six in the nave and five in the chancel, each series capped by a long line of early seventeenth-century battlements and its beautiful porch. It is one of the finest perpendicular churches in the country.

Wymondham Abbey, 1948. The marks of the cloisters and some of the ancillary buildings, once part of the demesne of the great abbey, may clearly be seen in the foreground. Its site was given in 1107 by William D'Albini as a priory for between ten and twenty Benedictine monks and a parish church. He made his priory subject to the great Abbey of St Albans (of which his brother was Abbot). He neglected to lay down the exact relationship of the parishioners to monks and this confusion led to many bitter quarrels until Wymondham was created an Abbey in its own right in 1449.

At the dissolution the monasteries in 1536 sections of the abbey were demolished and the parish was allowed to buy what was left, in particular the south aisle, which was to become their parish church. In 1549, after a rebellion led by local tanner Robert Kett and his brother William, during which they stormed the city of Norwich, one of the abbey church towers became a gibbet. The body of William Kett was hung from its tower as a warning against further insurrection from the townsfolk. This magnificent edifice still stands today, its great towers visible for miles around, one of the most famous landmarks on the skyline of Norfolk.

CWS Brush Factory, Wymondham, 1973. The Co-operative Wholesale Society's factory was opened on Chapel Lane in 1922. It followed on the tail of the Briton Brush Company, which took over the S.D. Page & Son Brush Factory on Lady Lane in 1920. In fact Wymondham has a long tradition of wood turnery, images of which – the spoon and spigot – appear on the town's coat of arms. The CWS Brush Factory, with its distinctive teepee-like wood piles, employed over 220 people at its height. Sadly it closed forever in January 1983 and was demolished in 1987–8. Today there is no more brush production in Wymondham. The area of this old factory has now been covered entirely by a housing estate.

Wymondham, viewed from above Fairland Street, 1932. The land which gave the street its name and where seasonal fairs are still held today is seen on the bottom right. Centre stage is the Market Cross. To the right of the cross is the King's Head Hotel (now demolished and the site occupied by Woolworths) and behind it is King's Head Meadow where the town's Whit Monday sports were held for generations. Although they no longer take place, sporting and social activities are still held here as it is the home ground of Wymondham Town Football Club.

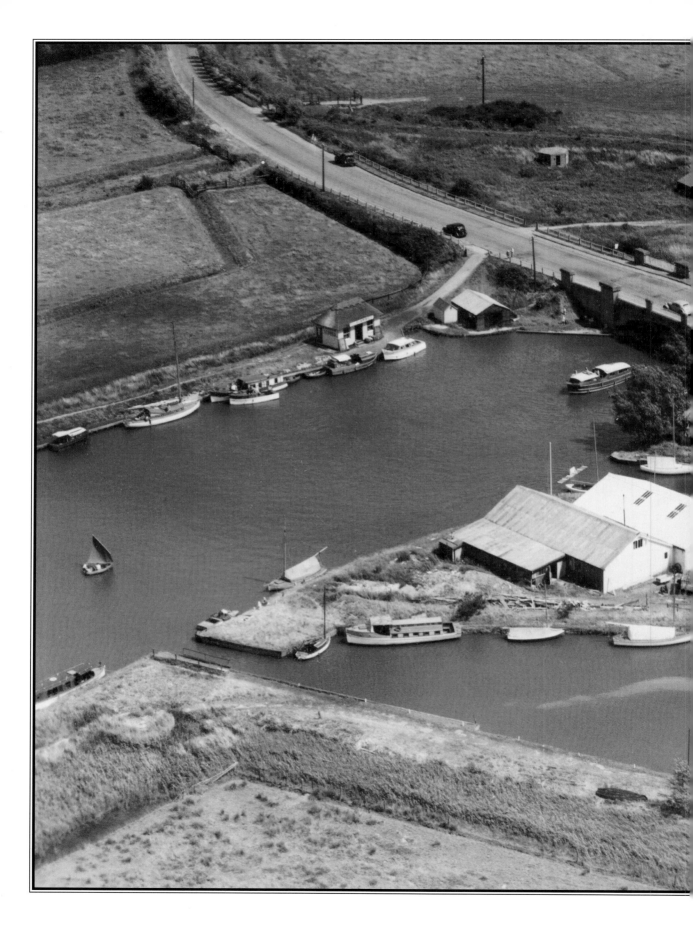

Waterways & Broads

Acle bridge and staithe, about 1 mile from the town, 1951. The original bridge was constructed from stone and consisted of three arches. It was known as Weybridge, deriving its name from the once nearby priory established by Roger Bigod during the reign of Edward I. The new single-arch bridge seen here was built in about 1930. It connects the old hundreds of Walsham and West Flegg and no other bridge existed between here and the mouth of the Yare for many years; there is now one other. It forms an important pass and has been viewed as a point of military significance. Plans were drawn up to fortify it as part of the county's defences during the armada scares of 1588 and during the Napoleonic Wars. The Home Guard was placed on sentry here during the Second World War and the Broads Flotilla plied the waters around with armed pleasure craft.

The River Yare sweeps in a wide curve past the boat yards and moorings at Brundall, 1969. At the beginning of the twentieth century the mighty black-sailed wherries had this waterway almost to themselves. In those days the inhabitants of Brundall numbered under 100. As the attraction of Norfolk's waterways and broads grew as a holiday destination for those who enjoy pleasurecraft and yachts, Brundall grew too. By 1931 its population numbered almost 1,000.

English Beet Sugar Corporation Factory, Cantley, 1928. Built in 1912 under the auspices of the Anglo-Netherlands Sugar Corporation Ltd, it was the first of its kind to open in the UK. Sadly the venture ran at a loss and was acquired by the English Beet Sugar Corporation Ltd during the First World War. The factory reopened in 1920 and has gone from strength to strength. Wherries served the factory from the river until 1950 and it had its own link to the Great Eastern Railway until 1960. The main mode of transport to the site is now by road on 'The Sugar Trail', no doubt familiar to any regular Norfolk road user. The factory has expanded and progressed with the times. Almost twenty other similar factories have been built subsequently all over the country. This one alone produces over 1 million tonnes every year.

An idyllic rural scene with a backdrop of the rich fen lands spreading as far as the eye can see is completed in the foreground by Denver Corn Windmill, photographed in 1954. This mill bears a date block marked 1835, but milling has been carried out here for considerably longer at earlier wooden post mills which stood on the site. Over the years steam, and later oil, engine milling were installed to complement wind power. However, in 1941 the mill was struck by lightning and wind power ceased. Grinding was carried on by diesel power but measures were taken to preserve the mill. It was signed over to Norfolk County Council by deed of gift in 1973 by Mrs Edith Staines after the death of her brother Thomas Edwin Harris, the last miller. The mill has been well restored and will be a familiar landmark for many years to come.

New Cut Bridge, Haddiscoe, 1961. Bisecting the picture is the final stretch of the New Cut constructed from the Yare at Reedham to join the Waveney at this junction. The river divides the counties, putting St Olave's, with its distinctive bowsprung girder bridge, in Suffolk and Haddiscoe in Norfolk. The cut was the brainchild of Alderman Crisp Brown and a group of Norwich merchants, who proposed turning Norwich into a port by constructing this navigation. The idea was formalised and William Cubbitt was appointed engineer.

The first parliamentary bill including details of the cut was presented in 1826 but met fierce opposition from the Yarmouth Corporation, which saw the potential loss of trade to Lowestoft. The Bill was defeated by a majority of five. A second Bill was presented and after a vigorous discussion it was passed on 28 May 1827. Great celebrations were held in Norwich and work began with haste. The Norwich and Lowestoft Navigation was opened to great acclaim on 30 September 1833.

It was sadly not to be the success predicted. Profits never really came. In 1842 the commissioners who had loaned money to the project took over ownership, and soon sold it to Sir Morton Peto who wished to eliminate competition to his railway, which provided comparatively cheap, quick and efficient trade routes across the country. Although many valiant attempts were made to reclaim the navigation, Norwich never became the envisaged port.

Horning, 1951. The village is set in 2,604 acres of marsh, once dotted with many windmills employed in pumping the water from the lowlands. It is surrounded by rich arable land and 50 acres of tidal waters and is one of the best known in Broadland. The village consists of two long and irregularly built streets (once two villages, Upper and Lower Street), lined by notable old houses, many of which are thatched and flint faced. The stone was no doubt supplied from the ruins of St Benet's Abbey and is complemented by Surlingham bricks. The gables and dormers of the Swan Inn, built in 1897, appear just above the centre of the picture. The reach of the river just above here is known as 'Cinder Ovens', because of the ovens that once lined the Woodbastwick side and produced coke for use in malt kilns up to the nineteenth century.

Potter Heigham, 1951. One of the centres of the broadland industry, the village has thriving boat-building yards, chalet estates and a caravan park. One name synonymous with the holiday boat trade is Herbert Woods Ltd. Based in the centre of the village, the firm is one of the biggest boat-building concerns on the Broads. Herbert founded his yard in the mid-1920s and built his first boat in his spare time while working for his father, Walter. By 1939 he had launched a stream of stylish and popular cruisers, and his fleet totalled forty-five motor cruisers and twenty yachts.

Ranworth Broad, 1961. Connected to the River Bure by Ranworth Dyke this was once one continuous sheet of water but it now consists of the open Malthouse Broad (seen here) and the closed Ranworth Inner Broad. Formerly a noted place for decoying, very large quantities of duck, teal and widgeon being captured during severe winters, the area is now preserved as part of the National Nature Reserve. Folklore tells that the ghost of Brother Pacificus may be seen rowing across this very water on moonlit nights to attend to the rood screen he restored in the nearby St Helen's Church.

Reedham, 1973. Sir Morton Peto promised the people of Lowestoft that if they would sell their harbour works and back him in making a railway, their mackerel and herrings would be delivered 'almost alive' in Manchester, Liverpool and London. They invested in his project and in 1847 the railway link was achieved, the most significant part of the project being the construction of the swing bridge over the Yare here at Reedham. It was built in 1846. This was the crossing that took the line over the water to Norwich and thus to the networks to the big cities Sir Morton had promised.

A motor cruiser swings out of Thurne dyke into the main river, 1951. The popularity of the dyke as a mooring for Broads visitors is the result not only of its fine marshland views but also its close proximity to the ancient Lion Inn in the village. To the left is Thurne Mill, which was built as a drainage mill following the enclosure of Thurne township in 1820. It was maintained initially on an *ad hoc* basis by marsh men until the drainage commissioners for East and West Flegg established a fee-paying system, whereby the landowners funded its upkeep. A familiar sight to Broads visitors, Thurne Mill still stands today. Owned by Mr R.D. Morse it is leased to the Norfolk Windmill Trust, which has scheduled it for major renovation over the next few years.

Wroxham and Hoveton St John, 1928. At the end of the nineteenth century young Arnold Roy established a business supplying provisions to broads visitors from a small shop in Coltishall. Enjoying success in this venture, he was joined by his brother and sister and they opened a new shop on a prime site near the river in Hoveton. The yard of John Loynes & Sons (bottom right) was already established as a boat-building and hire business and as demand for craft grew more boatyards joined in the growing industry. Roy's of Wroxham (as it was always known despite being in Hoveton) grew with them. By the time this photograph was taken Roy's had established additional shops at Potter Heigham and Horning and had begun to develop new premises around the village centre at its 'Wroxham' headquarters. Eventually the whole village centre was taken over by buildings owned by Roy's and housing various departments, including a pharmacy, drapery, ironmongery, fish stores and of course the grocery department in Arnold House. By the 1950s its proud boast was to be 'The largest Village Store in the World' and, still in family hands, it flourishes to this day.

The Coast

Coastline south-east of Cromer. Here the cliffs are made up of soft sandy deposits from the Ice Age. By the nature of their composition they are susceptible to collapse and they are certainly no defence against the ravages of the sea. All along this coastline from Cromer to Winterton towns, villages and valuable land have been swept away over the years. The rising cliffs of this particular stretch of coastline dramatically illustrate this point with the great 'bites' of cliff falls gorged out along their length. The area shown was the heart of 'Poppyland', its fields swayed with the distinctive red flowers. The symbolic centre of it all was the round tower of St Michaels' church, Sidestrand, near the cliff edge. Further along the coast was Foulness, a village which existed on a 2 mile spit of land out to sea. Further along, near Cromer, was the town of Shipden. All of these places and settlements in this short stretch have been totally lost to the sea.

Blakeney, 1971. Little remains of the great port built upon the rich trade in wool and fishing which flourished here in the Middle Ages. Later came the grain trade, but the tidal waters continually carried the spit of land at Blakeney Point farther west and consequently the channel silted up – until it is now 4 miles from the quayside to the open sea. Today the village is popular all year round; visitors walk in the salt marshes, the colours of which change through the seasons, or sail out from the quay in pleasurecraft. Most of the 600 houses in the village are now second homes or holiday lets. These, however, have been well restored and a comfortable character is retained in the village, with no small thanks to the Blakeney Neighbourhood Housing Society founded in 1946 by Norah Clogstoun.

Brancaster Staithe, 1972. This was an important and well-defended port in Roman times and not far from here was its fort, known then as Branodunum. From here Rome's British fleet protected the approaches to The Wash and its corn-growing hinterland. Just above centre right was the site of what was reputed to be the largest malthouse in England, measuring 312 feet long, 31 feet broad and capable of wetting 420 quarters of barley a week. Today Brancaster Staithe is a sleepy little coastal village bordered by sea, mud flat and marsh. It is still home to a few hardy souls who eke out a living from the North Sea, mostly from the mussel industry.

Burnham Deepdale, 1972. It was described by William White in his Norfolk directory of 1845 as 'a small village seated on a gentle acclivity above the surrounding salt marshes . . . sheltered on the south by a range of lofty hills finely clothed in wood'. Little has changed to spoil this area in over 100 years. The church of St Mary with its sturdy Saxon round tower is nationally renowned for its skilfully decorated Norman font, upon which are depicted the months of the year. It is remarkable that it survived, especially as it spent forty years of its life in the garden of Fincham rectory.

Burnham Deepdale is the most coastal of all the seven North Norfolk parishes known as 'The Burnhams'. They are now Burnham Deepdale, Norton, Overy, Sutton, Thorpe, Ulph and Westgate (or Market). The original seven were Burnham St Andrew, St Edmund, Norton, Overy, Sutton, Ulph and Westgate, all of these churches situated in a 1½ mile rectangle. St Andrew and St Edmund were absorbed long ago by Westgate and Overy respectively, to be replaced in the 'group' by the more distant Deepdale and Thorpe.

Caister-on-Sea, 1961. Although an intriguing feature on our coastline when viewed from the air, caravan sites and now rather dated holiday chalet camps have infected a coastline which remained unspoilt from the beginning of time until the opening years of the twentieth century. Now such sites may be viewed almost uninterruptedly from Great Yarmouth to Hemsby. Almost buried among the caravans is the historic town of Caister-on-Sea, founded in about AD 125 as a walled and well-defended Roman port over 30 acres. It had gradually declined to become a scattered village of about 900 inhabitants by the eighteenth century. Surrounded by 'rich loamy uplands . . . and a tract of fertile marshes', the area was drained by a steam engine erected in 1841. Just over 100 years later much of that land was taken up by the Great Yarmouth and Caister Golf Club and the early holiday camps. The latter grew rapidly, with the development of cheaper long distance railway travel, to accommodate holidaymakers, many from the north, who arrived at the Great Yarmouth stations by the trainload in the summer months.

Cley next the Sea, 1961. This is a beloved little unspoilt North Norfolk coastal village, complete with beautifully restored windmill and quality shops. Cley was once a bustling port and the custom house for Blakeney and Cley, situated here, sent returns in 1844 indicating that 38,000 quarters of corn and over 10,000 sacks of flour were exported and over 20,000 chaldrons of coal, 4 cargoes of timber and 14 cargoes of rape and linseed cake passed through the harbour. There were also custom house officials employed as collector, comptroller, clerk and tidewaiters. Sadly these were the last days of the grand old port. In the seventeenth century the marshes were embanked and this caused the channels gradually to silt up, because the tides were prevented from scouring them. The port had become 'landed up' by the end of the nineteenth century. Sitting quietly behind the sweeping salt marshes, the village has endured many battles with the sea, particularly during the east coast floods of 1953.

Cromer, 'Gem of the Norfolk Coast', 1928. A bathing centre from the early nineteenth century, it was popularised by Clement Scott's articles about 'Poppyland' in the *Daily Telegraph* during the 1880s and 1890s. Then with the coming of the railway the sleepy fishing village expanded to become a very fashionable destination for Victorian and Edwardian daytrippers and holidaymakers. The whole shape of the town changed as the great hotels were built. Two stations served Cromer and even a horse-drawn liveried coach ferried visitors to the best establishments. Although the High Street area of Cromer received considerable bomb damage during the Second World War, much of the town retains that same Victorian charm today. Extending out to sea is the 183 yard pier built in 1899 for £11,000. Not far from the end of the pier is Church Rock, said to be the last remnant of the town of Shipden whose phantom bells are said to boom eerily from under the waves when a storm is brewing.

Great Yarmouth, 1922. St Nicholas' church, claimed as the largest parish church in England and set in 8 acres in the north-east corner of the town, was built in the early twelfth century by Herbert de Losinga, Bishop of Norwich. It replaced the earlier Saxon church of St Benet which stood on the site.

The magnificent church's spire took its total height up to 186 feet (see page 136). It fell into decay from the seventeenth century onwards but restoration work began in the mid-nineteenth century. Beyond the church to the left is the Primitive Methodist chapel (Yarmouth Temple) on Priory Plain built in 1875. It had seating for 1,200 people but was demolished in the early 1970s to make way for the town's inner link road. On the right is Church Plain, known locally as Brewery Plain after Lacon's brewery which spreads along the far right side; its chimney is just visible.

Great Yarmouth, 1922. Here, just coming off Breydon Water, is the junction where the River Bure (right) meets the River Yare, which forges the main passage through the docks to the sea. At the bottom left is the North Quay bridge, built along with the railway in 1847; it linked the railway with the quayside tramway. It was improved to become a suspension bridge in the 1880s. The area behind the quay known as Middlegate, including Rainbow Square and Laughing Image corner, was badly damaged during the 1941–2 blitz; what was left after the bombing was almost totally destroyed by postwar development. Note the old Haven Bridge, which once marked the county boundary. To the right of the river is Southtown or 'Little Yarmouth', which was officially in Suffolk until 1891 when the boundaries were changed.

Great Yarmouth, 1920. Running like tram tracks across the centre of the photograph are the parallel roads of Middlegate Street (right) and King Street. Between these roads was the Middlegate area of Great Yarmouth – the heart of the famous old 'Rows' of houses. Hundreds of families were crammed into 145 of these narrow passages, which varied in width from 3 to 6 feet although at one point on Row 95 the gap was only 27 inches wide. This was a community in its own right with churches, chapels, shops, schools and thirty-three pubs within its bounds. Most of the area was destroyed during the air raids of 1941–2. Opposite this area, just behind St Peter's church, the first civilian casualties caused by dropping bombs were incurred during the first Zeppelin air raid on 19 January 1915.

Great Yarmouth, 1928. The town centre with empty marketplace extending to the right. In the top left we can see the temporary bridge and the works to construct the new Haven Bridge. The fine colonnaded building to the centre left is Arnolds Ltd drapery, house furnishing and china stores. Moving down the photograph we find Regent Road. At the top of the street on the left is the large, square Wesleyan Methodist chapel opposite that is the Theatre Royal. Erected in 1778, remodelled in 1820 and further improved in the 1890s it was capable of seating audiences of up to 1,000. This was demolished and replaced in succession by the Regal Theatre and Cinematograph Hall, the ABC Theatre and finally the Cannon cinema, which was also flattened in the late 1980s to make way for some shops. The area behind the theatre toward Market Gates is now the Market Gates shopping centre.

Great Yarmouth, 1953. This is the Haven Bridge and beyond it the familiar frontages on Hall Quay. The new road layout, complete with roundabout, made in 1929–30. Note in the middle distance the chimney and works buildings of Grout's Silk Factory on St Nicholas Road. To the left of the photograph we can see the beginning of clearance and postwar development of the badly bomb damaged areas. This reconstruction worked its way from Church Plain to the 'Rows' of Middlegate and flattened everything to make way for car parks, council housing and flats.

Great Yarmouth, 19 November 1953. The tragic shell of St Nicholas' church photographed ten years almost to the day after it was reduced to ruins by the hail of fire bombs dropped on the town. Rebuilding began in 1957 under the architect Stephen Dykes-Bower. Sadly the funds could not run to rebuilding of the spire but the rest was sympathetically and skilfully reconstructed. Pews, tester and organ came from redundant churches. The most notable part of the rebuilding programme is probably the St Andrew's chapel iron screen. Designed by Dykes-Bower, it is 19 feet high, weighs about 15 tons and took Eric Stephenson of Wroxham five years to make. The church was reconsecrated and officially reopened on 8 May 1961.

Great Yarmouth, 1961. Seen here is 'The Barracks' housing estate. Built in 1925 as corporation housing, it faithfully retains the shape of the old artillery barracks and South Star battery upon which it was built. In the foreground is the world-famous Great Yarmouth Pleasure Beach, begun in 1909. For many years only three rides were allowed on the site – the scenic railway, the caves under the scenic railway and 'The Joy Wheel'. The park was then allowed to develop but the original wooden scenic railway burnt down in 1919. Rebuilt in 1932, it survives today as one of the oldest all wooden scenic railways in the world. This photograph shows the Pleasure Beach with many new features built by the Botton Brothers after they acquired it in 1954. It is still in their hands today.

Great Yarmouth, 1969. Northgate Hospital began life in 1837 as the new town workhouse with room for 400 paupers. In 1894 and 1898 this old building was improved and enlarged to become the Great Yarmouth Isolation Hospital 'for all kind of infectious diseases'. It had beds for eighty patients. The accommodation for nurses was increased and improved in 1907 and further extensions were built over the years, the last being the maternity unit (the large white block on the left). Known for a short while as the Estcourt Hospital, after the road on which it stands, today it is known as the Northgate Hospital and is used exclusively for psychiatric patients.

Great Yarmouth Grammar School was founded in 1551, closed in 1757, and re-established by local charity trustees under a scheme put in place by the Court of Chancery in 1862. Expansion was necessary and in 1910 the school moved to purpose-built premises, costing £7,625, on Salisbury Road. The new building comprised an assembly hall for 250 boys, with organ chamber, eleven large classrooms, art room, science lecture room, laboratories, library, manual workshop and porter's lodge. The school was extended in 1937 and again in 1957.

Great Yarmouth, 1969. The view from Haven Bridge along South Quay to the South Denes where the Yare, swelled with the converging waters of the Bure, Waveney and their tributaries, flows into the North Sea. The north side of the ancient channel to the sea was called Grubb's Haven. This became choked with sand, the southern channel near Corton followed suit and by 1337 the trade of the town was stopped. Desperate attempts were made to cut new channels, but all failed until the Netherlands engineer Joas Johnson cut his channel between 1559 and 1567. This watercourse, defended by jetties and piers was described by Daniel Defoe as 'The finest Quay in England if not in Europe'. It still serves the port today.

Heacham, 1971. This view shows St Mary's church with its 600-year-old tower and looks across Heacham Park and on to Redgate Hill. The hall (just above centre left) was home to generations of the Rolfe family, including John Rolfe, the adventurer who explored the Americas. When he was Governor of Virginia he married Princess Pochahontas. They eventually came to Norfolk and lived for some time at the old family home of Heacham Hall. Down the road towards Snettisham is Caley Mill, the home of Norfolk Lavender Ltd. Founded by Linn Chilvers in 1932, it is the last full-scale lavender farm in England.

Happisburgh, 1961. Rising above the neat and historic village, which includes many thatched cottages, is the church of St Mary. Its 110 foot towers are emphasised by the eminence upon which the whole church stands and it is visible for miles around. Not surprisingly this tower was the part on which the first guide beacon was lit to guide shipping past the treacherous waters just beyond the village. In 1791 two lights, one 80 feet and the other 100 feet tall were erected. Known as the high and low lights and lit by patent reflectors, they were red and could be seen up to 17 miles out to sea. At the north end of the Newarp Sand was a floating light carrying three lamps and a flag. A gong was sounded here in times of fog. Before we leave Happisburgh look to the right of the photograph and admire Happisburgh Manor, 'an advanced building' with its central rectangular block and diagonally projecting wings. It was built by Detmar Blow in 1900.

Newport, Hemsby, 1974. Here we see more of the almost continuous coastline bungalow-chalet-caravan chain from Great Yarmouth. Newport is part of the old 1,627-acre parish of Hemsby and was once mostly fields. The ancient manor was part of the demesne of Norwich Cathedral for the prior claimed homage of the tenants and gave two palfreys to have a market during the reign of Henry III (1216–72). After Edward I ascended the throne he claimed here 'wreck at sea, view of frankpledge, assize, free-warren, pillory and tumbrel'. A few bungalows constructed on stilts were built shortly after the beginning of the twentieth century in the dunes here. Little changed until the 1950s when the demands of a growing holiday trade spread. Gradually caravan parks were constructed and holiday camps appeared, complete with their own bingo halls, swimming pools and allied accoutrements enclosed with barbed wire. These have now replaced the rich fields of swaying crops.

Hunstanton, 1950. Known to many as 'Sunny Hunny', this has been a popular seaside resort since the 1860s when, with the coming of the railway, Hamon Le Strange began to develop New Hunstanton as a pleasure resort. The new town was designed by William Butterfield, the well-known church architect. By 1890 the population had more than doubled and was described in White's directory as now having 'whole streets and terraces of commodious lodging and boarding houses and several first class hotels; and many villas, shops and private residences'. Extending 800 feet out to sea is the pier, built in 1870, its glory now lost to the past through storm damage in 1979, economics and erosion.

Hunstanton lighthouse, 1920. Along the cliffs that rise to 65 feet above the beach is St Edmund's Point; tradition has it that St Edmund the Martyr landed here after his journey from Germany to be crowned King of East Anglia. The ruins of the fifteenth-century chapel built in his honour may be seen to the right. Nearby on this eminence was Hunstanton lighthouse. The original wooden lighthouse contained the world's first parabolic reflector and was built here in 1776 by Edward Everard. The old lighthouse structure was replaced by this sturdier building completed by Trinity House in 1830. Its occulting light atop the 50 foot tower could be seen up to 16 miles out to sea on a clear night. Sadly, the light was dismantled a few years after this photograph was taken.

King's Lynn, 1928. Centre stage in this photograph is the Tuesday marketplace and St Nicholas' church, part of the 'Newland' of the town, which dates back to the twelfth century. Here public punishments were administered, the pillory was situated and witches were burnt at the stake. The 800-year-old Lynn Mart begins every year on the square on St Valentine's Day. The square is enclosed by many fine late seventeenth- and eighteenth-century houses. One of them, just to the right, may be identified by its distinctive cartouche as the Duke's Head Inn. It was built on the site of the old Griffin Inn in 1685 by John Turner from designs by Henry Bell. Another of Bell's designs, the market cross, stood in the centre of the market-place; it was taken down in 1831.

King's Lynn, 1932. Viewed across the River Great Ouse this is the oldest area of the town, where the first fishing and farming settlement known as Lin, Lenne or Leuna was founded. Many significant ancient buildings such as Hampton Court, the Hanseatic Warehouse and Thoresby College may be found here. Just below the centre of the photograph is the entrance of the ancient water course known as the Millfleet; further to the right is Boal Quay and the Greenland Fishery.

King's Lynn, 1952. This is the 1,000 feet long and 400 feet wide Bentinck Dock. Covering a water area of 10 acres, it was begun in 1881 and was opened to traffic in May 1884. It was eventually surrounded by three-quarters of a mile of branch railway. Today the whole area has been opened up into a spacious industrial area. All the old warehouses were demolished by 1973 and new silos and modern warehouses have been built in their place.

A commanding prospect of the town of King's Lynn and the village of West Lynn, separated by the River Great Ouse, 1969. No doubt a settlement has been here since before the Norman Conquest. By the thirteenth century the combined trade of Lynn and Boston (over the border in Lincolnshire) were reckoned to be greater than that of London. Sadly the port went slowly into decline as trading demands changed. By the early years of Queen Victoria's reign (1837–1901) the town was in decay. The Victorians' zest for improvement and change fuelled the rebuilding of many of the town's fortunes. From the 1920s sweeping changes were made to the town's layout. Many of the decayed Victorian slums and warehouses were cleared. The district of Gaywood was embraced within the town's boundaries in 1935. In the 1960s the town set about a controversial modernisation programme which produced the shopping complex around the Broad Street area and housing developments of Columbia Way and Hillingdon Square. At the 1991 census the population was 36,000.

King's Lynn, 1971. Surrounded by the modern open spaces of car parks we see the historic heart of old King's Lynn around the Saturday marketplace. The stately cruciform church of St Margaret was founded by Herbert de Losinga, the first Bishop of Norwich, in 1101 as part of a Benedictine Priory. It is distinguished by its two 82 foot towers. An impressive building it measures 235 feet long and has a central lantern rising 132 feet; it is renowned for its two magnificent Flemish brasses. To the left of St Margaret's is the familiar façade of the Town Hall. It was built as the hall of the wealthy merchant guild of the Holy Trinity in 1423 after fire destroyed its predecessor. Behind the main hall are two more; the Assembly and Card Rooms built in 1767. Most of the front of the building houses the mayor's parlour and municipal offices, added in 1895.

Mundesley, 1965. Once a quiet fishing village resting on the lofty North Norfolk cliffs, it has been a popular bathing place since the beginning of the nineteenth century. However, like so many villages on this stretch of coastline, it fights a consistent battle against the erosion of the cliffs by the sea. The high tides and gales in 1836, 1845 and 1862 did particular damage. When the village was being reconstructed after the storm damage in 1845 Francis Wheatley Esq., the Deputy Vice-Admiral of the coast, enacted many improvements in the village and built his great mansion, Cliff House. At a cost of £1,000 he constructed two massive walls to form an upper and lower terrace up to 90 feet above the beach in an attempt to defend his new home from the sea; those walls, after numerous rebuilds, have gone but Cliff House still stands today. Mundesley, although never enjoying the same popularity as Cromer, was popularised as a seaside resort when the Norfolk & Suffolk Joint Railway built the loop linking North Walsham, Mundesley and Overstrand to Cromer in the late nineteenth century. Sadly the line was not the success it was anticipated to be and less than a year after the trains ceased in 1964 the station and 12 acres of railway land were sold for £12,150. Today just about all traces of the railway line, the station, its land and the market garden in the foreground have disappeared. The area is now covered by a housing development.

Mundesley Holiday Camp, 1961. In 1823 it was proposed that a spa should be created in Mundesley. People could come to 'take waters' from the limpid spring which 'effected extraordinary cures' in those affected by chronic rheumatic, scrofulous and scrobatic diseases. The spa village did not emerge but people did enjoy the fine beach and air. The creation of hotels and conversion of inns to larger hostelries had begun by the end of the nineteenth century. The holiday potential of the area was recognised by entrepreneur Victor Edwards who constructed this, the first, purpose-built, fully self-catering holiday camp in Norfolk. The distinctive shape of the camp is both artistic and practical; its layout is an interpretation of the sails of Paston Mill. Being situated on the hilltop just behind the cliffs, the camp looks inland and not out to sea. The idea behind the camp was to create something totally different for the family holiday. A self-contained holiday centre, it initially had 172 chalets and capacity for 360 holiday-makers. There was piped cold water to all chalets but hot water had to be obtained from central taps. Greatly improved and modernised since its foundation, the Mundesley Holiday Centre is still operating today.

Salthouse, 1971. This is an ancient settlement surrounded by Bronze Age burial mounds and barrows which may be observed behind the church. Salthouse was another Glaven Port (the name given to a number of ports along the course of the River Glaven and its tributaries). It rested on an arm of the sea which connected it to the Mayne Channel coming up from Blakeney and Cley. Like its counterparts Salthouse had its channel blocked up by the collapsing embankments of the seventeenth and eighteenth centuries. The sea has certainly determined the fate of the village in many ways over the years. The vulnerable marshes, drained and embanked in 1863, have been breached many times – seriously in 1863 and horrifically in 1953 during the east coast floods, when a number of properties were swept away or severely damaged and people died.

Sheringham, 1926. This smartly built Victorian town was developed from a sleepy fishing village after the coming of the railway in 1887. The old line, with level-crossing over the entrance road to the town, signal-box, passenger bridge and goods yard, may be observed to the bottom right. The old station is now headquarters of the North Norfolk Railway and the goods yard is a car park where a Saturday market is also held.

Snettisham, 1971. Snettisham is a pleasant, unspoilt village, familiar to the many visitors who pass its carstone frontages and 175 foot spired church of St Mary on their journey down the coast road between Hunstanton and King's Lynn. Over the years the lands around the village have yielded much of value. In the parish there were once chalk pits and carstone quarries, which supplied local builders for generations. Without doubt, however, the greatest treasures are the ancient tools, coins and artefacts found in the local fields, most notable of all being the gold alloy torc found by ploughman Tom Rout at Ken Hill in November 1950. This important find, along with other objects uncovered later in the area, is now in the British Museum, London. Much to the chagrin of many Norfolk people the torcs have only been on public display in the county once since their discovery fifty years ago.

Wells-next-the-Sea, 1950. This town, built in an irregular grid pattern, owes its existence, wealth and structure to its relationship with the sea. The wealth of the port was built on the wool trade and later came the export of corn and oysters and imports of coal, timber, rape, linseed cakes, fertilisers and, most importantly, malt. Great improvements were begun on the old port town in 1859 when the Earl of Leicester built the embankment due north from the west end of the quay, thereby straightening the once tortuous channel that had forced ships to discharge their loads into small boats in the pool by the lighthouse. Further improvements came in the 1860s after the Local Government Act whereby gas works were erected in Park Road, streets and roads were improved and a stone quay of 250 yards in length was erected at a total cost of £23,000. In the coniferous forest towards the sea is a large boating lake known as Abraham's Busom, which was created as a result of the embankment; all the old creeks which had run westward in this former 'arm of the sea' were cut off and formed this lake. Seen here, probably at its best, the lake and trees were all swept away by the 1953 floods. The town was also severely affected and many dramatic rescues were required. Both the town and Abraham's Bosom have been reconstructed, but of course it takes far longer for trees to grow than for bricks and mortar to be repaired.

Weybourne, 1962. The charming village of Weybourne rests in the centre of a natural basin surrounded by plantations and heath. An ancient couplet exclaims, 'He that would old England win, Must at Weybourne Hope begin,' and very true it is. The beach runs steeply into the sea to form a natural harbour and consequently it has been a prime target for any prospective invasion force since the Vikings. Here among ancient remnants of fortifications was the Board of Trade coast guard station on the cliff top: armed with life-saving apparatus they kept a silent vigil over the icy waters for many years.

Winterton-on-Sea, 1962. In the nineteenth century Winterton Ness was well known to mariners as 'the most fatal headland between Scotland and London'. For many years a Trinity House light served the coastline but before that there were two lights on the Ness and a floating light in the Cockle Gatt at the north entrance to Yarmouth Road. A coastguard, lighthouse keeper, beach men and a pilot were all stationed here.

Eighty Years of Aerial Excellence

Aerofilms is a thriving commercial enterprise with a fleet of three aircraft fitted with state-of-the-art cameras. The company remains at the forefront of new technology in the sphere of aerial photography and surveying and is committed to the constant renewal of its aerial archive.

The Aerofilms library today holds over two million aerial photographs, dating from 1919 to the present day. The major part of the collection is taken up with UK photography. This includes historic black and white and modern colour photography which captures the face of Britain in the twentieth century. The archive also includes a fascinating collection of international aerial photography from the 1950s and '60s covering the Americas, Europe, Asia, Antarctica and Africa, and Mills Collection, a unique record of Victorian London.

The Aerofilms collection comprises both vertical survey photography and oblique photography. Vertical photography has many uses, including mapping, surveying and land use. Oblique photography is excellent for display or publishing purposes. All photography is available as photographic prints, transparencies or scanned as digital files on cd-rom. Map accurate, rectified imagery is available through Aerofilms' Orthophoto Department.

All existing photography is easily available from the Aerofilms library. Details of specific areas of interest can be faxed or posted and a search will be carried out for relevant views. For clients with exact specifications Aerofilms can be commissioned to take new oblique or vertical photography at competitive prices.

Aerofilms is currently in the midst of a project to provide complete aerial photographic coverage of England ready for the millennium. The Millennium Aerial Photographic Survey (MAPS) by UK Perspectives will be captured in 1999 at 1:10,000 scale and produced digitally to a mapping specification to become the definitive base line data set.

AEROFILMS
LIMITED

Phone: 0181 207 0666
Fax: 0181 207 5433
E-Mail: library@Aerofilms.com
Gate Studios Station Road Borehamwood Hertfordshire WD6 1EJ